STORIES BEHIND THE TRADITIONS AND SONGS of EASTER

Other Books by Ace Collins

Turn Your Radio On:
The Stories Behind Gospel Music's
All-Time Greatest Songs

Stories Behind the Best-Loved Songs of Christmas

Stories Behind the Hymns That Inspire America

Stories Behind the Great Traditions of Christmas

I Saw Him in Your Eyes:
Everyday People Making Extraordinary Impact

More Stories Behind the
Best-Loved Songs of Christmas

STORIES BEHIND THE
TRADITIONS
AND SONGS
of
EASTER

ACE COLLINS
BESTSELLING AUTHOR

ZONDERVAN®

ZONDERVAN.com/
AUTHORTRACKER
follow your favorite authors

Stories Behind the Traditions and Songs of Easter
Copyright © 2007 by Andrew Collins

Requests for information should be addressed to:

Zondervan, *Grand Rapids, Michigan 49530*

Library of Congress Cataloging-in-Publication Data
    Collins, Ace.
       Stories behind the traditions and songs of Easter / Ace Collins.
          p. cm.
      ISBN-10: 0-310-26315-8 (alk. paper)
      ISBN-13: 978-0-310-26315-9 (alk. paper)
       1. Easter. 2. Public worship. 3. Easter music—History and criticism. 4.
    Hymns—History and criticism. I. Title.
    BV55.C64 2007
    263'.93—dc22

                                      2006025105

This edition printed on acid-free paper.

Interior design by Pam Eicher

Printed in the United States of America

07 08 09 10 11 12 • 20 19 18 17 16 15 14 13 12 11 10 9 8 7 6 5 4 3 2

Special thanks to:

Bill Gaither

John Hillman

Kathy Collins

Angela Scheff

Steve Morse

CONTENTS

INTRODUCTION

The History of the Easter Celebration

The four gospels not only record the events of what is now known as the first Easter but also bring insight into the emotional impact of those events on the followers of Christ. From the initial sadness brought on by his death on the cross, to the disbelief about his return to life, to the jubilation that came with the acceptance of his resurrection, the first Easter was one those who witnessed it would never forget. Yet strangely, even though the events of that time were recorded in detail by four different biblical authors, none of these men set down the date when it happened.

There can be little doubt that for at least the next two or three decades Easter was observed by those who witnessed the events in Jerusalem. They probably worshiped and gave thanks on the anniversaries of the crucifixion and resurrection. Yet there are no records of what those worship services were like. What can be gleaned from history is that many who first accepted Christ as Savior were persecuted, and so they would have kept their celebrations hidden. Those early Christians who were able to worship freely were probably more intent on living a Christlike life. To these believers, Jesus' death and resurrection were remembered daily and were part of every facet of their worship.

As Christianity spread and the events of Christ's life on earth became more distant, believers began to mark certain days as

important moments in church history. Because Christ's resurrection is the foundation of the Christian faith, it is only natural that early believers would set aside a time to remember Christ's life, death, and resurrection and to reflect on what they meant to them both as individuals and as a body of believers. Irenaeus of Lyon wrote in the second century that Christians often fasted between sundown on a specified Friday until sunrise on the following Sunday. Though no name was ascribed to this tradition, this is probably the earliest historical record of what is now known as Easter. What Irenaeus observed was probably not a solitary tradition established by a particular group of Christians he knew but rather one that was echoed throughout the now far-flung Christian community.

While no clearly established moment in time can be ascertained, reports from Irenaeus and other historians seem to show that Easter has been celebrated longer than any other Christian holiday. But since there was no date marked in the Bible, the weekend set aside to memorialize this special moment in history was not universal. Most early churches chose springtime because of the connection with Passover. Some even called the Easter weekend the "Days of Pascha," meaning Passover. Yet no one, not Paul, Timothy, nor any of their followers, would have called it Easter. In fact, the word Easter cannot be found in the Bible, and the term's roots are most likely anchored anywhere but in holy ground.

At about the same time that Irenaeus wrote of Christians marking Christ's death and resurrection, missionaries began to travel out of the Holy Land, Rome, and Greece into Northern Europe. As these early pioneers of the Great Commission converted members of the Teutonic tribes, they were confronted

by long-held traditions that were opposed to the values of the Christian faith. To these men of God, these old customs offered a real challenge. Going back centuries, the ritual celebrations were deeply ingrained in the culture of these new believers. Yet they also were meant to honor some of the myriad pagan gods that these people had worshiped. The missionaries knew that if they forbade all established celebrations, they might face a revolt that would cripple their ministry. These godly men also recognized that these poor people needed celebrations to bring joy to their often bleak lives. So the missionaries worked out a compromise that would ultimately become a part of the way Christ's resurrection would be celebrated around the world.

To those living in the British Isles and Northern Europe, winter was a trying time. The days were long and cold. Each year, due to frigid temperatures, lack of food, and rampant disease, many died during this season. So when the snow and dark days gave way to flowers and warmer weather, these people believed it was a time for celebration dedicated to the gods or goddesses of spring, fertility, and the rising sun. In some of these Teutonic cultures, a month-long holiday was declared because the goddess Eostre (one of many spring gods and goddesses) had again brought the warm days of spring. Because of this goddess, every person had new life and hope. Knowing they would be unable to stop the actual pagan spring custom, the missionaries simply converted the holiday as they converted the men and women. Thus, the celebration of Eostre became Easter, and the new life celebrated was no longer a gift of pagan gods but rather a natural transformation to the rebirth guaranteed to Christians through Christ's ultimate sacrifice.

As missionaries spread the Good News across Europe and Asia, they discovered similar pagan gods that legend claimed were at least in part responsible for the new life that appeared each spring. The Phoenicians had Astarte, which as it crossed throughout Europe had morphed into Astarte and Ostara. As they had in Northern Europe, missionaries continued to use the customs of the people's history as a basis for the resurrection celebration. Thus the name Easter, likely derived from the name of the Teutonic pagan goddess, became the most common term for this new holiday.

Although millions of Christians now recognized it, there was still no set date for this special weekend. Thus for more than three centuries, Easter Sunday was celebrated at scores of different times depending on when the warm winds of spring began to blow or when the Jewish Passover was celebrated.

In 325, the leaders of a now tightly organized church felt the Christian calendar needed structure. Without set dates, it was hard to control the manner in which believers celebrated the various holidays. So the church hierarchy met in what is now known as the Council of Nicaea. At this meeting the leaders decided on certain edicts and gave their report to Emperor Constantine. Since Constantine was now a Christian and the world's most powerful ruler, the council knew his decrees would carry great weight with the Christian population. Two of the leader's pronouncements announced the setting of official dates for Christmas and Easter.

Christmas Day was set as December 25. Since this was the time when Roman cultures already celebrated the winter solstice, this date was chosen in an attempt to put a religious spin on the ancient holiday.

But Easter was more of a challenge. Since at least part of the church celebrated Easter in conjunction with Passover, it was deemed that this connection should be continued. Since Passover was observed in the spring, this would also connect with the times many other Christian groups celebrated Easter. Yet as Passover moved from year to year in conjunction with the cycle of the moon, the council did not feel it could set aside one spring weekend for Easter. Instead, they opted to embrace a date based on Jewish customs. Thus Easter became a mobile holiday.

The new law stated that Easter would be celebrated on the first Sunday after the first full moon after the vernal equinox. The full moon in the council's ruling was the ecclesiastical full moon, which was defined as the fourteenth day of a tabular lunation. Therefore, Easter would be celebrated on a Sunday between the dates of March 22 and April 25.

In Constantine's day, many depended on the cycles of the moon to determine when to plant, herd, and even travel. Additionally, Jews had been using this lunar system for centuries to determine when to mark Passover. So in the fourth century, figuring when Easter would fall each year was something most clergymen, farmers, shepherds, and tradesmen considered an elementary equation. Today, in a world in which few note the moon's cycles, this moving of Easter causes many Christians great confusion.

After 325, most of the world celebrated Christ's resurrection on the same day. It was also now universally recognized by the name Easter. Except for the addition of specific customs, few things changed about the holiday until the Reformation, when some of the new Protestant denominations attempted to erase all Christian holidays. They felt that both Christmas and Easter

contained more pagan elements than spiritual values. Hence in nations such as England and America, Easter was rarely mentioned by the press or celebrated by most Protestant churches. In 1840, Queen Victoria married Germany's Prince Albert, and the royal family, using long-held German customs, restored the Christian holidays of Christmas and Easter in England. Americans soon followed this lead. By the last half of the nineteenth century, Easter had become an important holiday weekend throughout the Christian world.

Unlike Christmas, Easter is not universally celebrated, nor has it been so deeply commercialized. The fact that it is a weekend that begins by remembering an innocent man's gruesome execution undoubtedly had something to do with it. And unlike at Christmas, gift-giving has no spiritual connection to the historical events of the first Easter. What probably has kept the heart of this celebration so focused on the spiritual rather than the commercial is the edict that deemed that Easter would not be set on a specific day. Because Easter moves each year, commercial connections cannot be as easily cemented as they can at Christmas. Therefore there is no specific Easter shopping period, no annual countdown of the days until Easter Sunday, and no real anchor that gives businesses the wedge they need to fully exploit this initially solemn but ultimately joyful occasion. Hence, even though its name is likely based on a long-forgotten pagan goddess, this oldest Christian holiday is also probably the purest and most spiritual. Each year Easter welcomes spring, new life, and new hope. More than decorated eggs or little bunnies is at the heart of the holiday's message. On Easter, we remember what the world was given when the first believers rolled back the stone and discovered that Christ lives!

All Glory, Laud, and Honor

*E*aster music was being written more than a thousand years ago. Even in the early church, monks composed scripturally based songs for use during the forty days of Lent and the Easter weekend. Though few of these early efforts have survived, there can be little doubt the ancient praise anthems offered great inspiration to the worshipers of their day.

Written around 820, "All Glory, Laud, and Honor" is probably the oldest Easter hymn still commonly sung by Christians. Because of its uplifting music and positive message, most of us don't know that this song of praise and hope was composed in a dark prison cell by a man who knew he would never emerge from within its walls. Our still knowing and singing this hymn today is due to the tireless study of this isolated man, a person deemed unfit for public service by the leaders of his church. So the story behind this magnificent hymn is a testament to God's ability to bring people of faith together and to use these people in a mighty fashion no matter how isolated they are. Though separated by a thousand years, two men, intimately connected

by their unswerving devotion to their Lord, paved the way for the world's most powerful Palm Sunday anthem.

If ever a man listened to Christ's directives and took them to heart, it was Theodulph of Orleans. Born in 760 in Italy, Theodulph was of royal blood. As a child he enjoyed wealth and protection not afforded to most people during those times. Theodulph also had the benefits of education and a staff of servants at his beck and call. In today's language, he had it made. Yet despite living in a world that demanded nothing of him, Theodulph heard a call stronger than the lure of luxury and power. After reading Jesus' challenge to the rich young man, Theodulph gave up his money, property, and title and surrendered his life to the Lord's service.

Overnight the former nobleman joined the ranks of the commoner as a priest. In this capacity he sought out the poorest of the poor, feeding them while he shared the story of Christ's birth, life, death, and resurrection. His devotion to "the least of these" made him incredibly popular with the region's people and an enigma to the royals whose lifestyle he had once shared. Yet just as these men and women of privilege did not forget Theodulph, he did not forget them. In fact, he constantly looked to them for the funding needed to provide for those in dire circumstances.

As he continued his mission in God's service, Theodulph migrated to a monastery in Florence, Italy. The twenty-one-year-old priest's passion for living out Christ's directives toward the poor caught the eye of one of the world's most powerful men. Charlemagne ordered Theodulph to come to his castle. After their meeting, the ruler appointed the priest as the Bishop of Orleans and moved him to France. Though again affiliated with the ruling class, Theodulph still devoted most of his time

to the sick, the orphans, the poor, and the lost. For the next thirty-seven years, Theodulph was the bridge between the royal family and the country's poor.

Because of Theodulph's influence, Charlemagne took an interest in not just feeding the people of his kingdom but educating them. Under Theodulph's guidance, priests across France set up schools devoted to teaching the children of poor families. For the first time, common people enjoyed a privilege once reserved for only the elite. Such was his status that Theodulph had only to ask, and the financing for God's work was set in motion. Yet when Charlemagne died, Theodulph, who had so closely followed the steps of Christ, found his life suddenly mirroring that of Paul.

France's new ruler, Louis the Pious, was intimidated by Theodulph's power. He felt the bishop's popularity and influence might challenge his own authority, so he charged Theodulph with treason and ordered him to spend the remainder of his days in prison. The bishop was now in his late fifties. Unable to reach out to the poor he so deeply loved, he turned to those who had also lost their freedom. They became his flock. As he shared the gospel with these men, a fact became clear in his mind. The king who had imprisoned him was nothing more than a figurehead. The only real King was the one he had served since the day he had given up his title and possessions. Power was therefore not in the royal castle but in the hearts of all who believed in Christ as King. So, he reasoned, even in prison, he was still a powerful man.

In his cell, Theodulph picked up a quill and wrote his revelation in verse form. It would not only be his greatest message but also his most lasting. He taught his new song to those around him. From behind the walls he and those who worshiped with

him sang out "All Glory, Laud, and Honor" with such strength and passion even the king was able to hear it.

Less than a year after writing his beautiful tribute to Christ, the bishop died. Most historians believe Louis the Pious sensed he could not quench the people's love and devotion for Theodulph by simply incarcerating him, so the only option left was to kill him. Though the good bishop was surely poisoned, "All Glory, Laud, and Honor" did not die with him. The hymn survived in his writings and was passed on to churches across Europe. Thus, even though the messenger was silenced, his message was not.

John Mason Neale was born in London, England, almost a thousand years after Theodulph died. The son of an Anglican priest, Neale studied at Trinity College, where he was recognized as one of the greatest writers in the distinguished school's history. After his graduation, Neale continued his education at Downing College, then he entered the clergy. Church leaders felt the young man was indeed brilliant, but they feared his theology was far too similar to the Catholic Church's theology for him to be trusted with a parish, so Neale was appointed the warden of a home for old men in East Grinstead. In this seemingly dead-end position, Neale established dynamic missions for orphans and prostitutes, made vast contributions to church music, and published works that greatly influenced worship in the Anglican Church.

Though he worked tirelessly to fulfill his mission duties, Neale also found time each day to study medieval church history and liturgy. Much of what Neale uncovered had been lost for hundreds of years. When he found writings that could speak to the modern church, he translated the documents into English. As he discovered sermons and writings, he also found

All Glory, Laud, and Honor

All glory, laud, and honor
To thee, Redeemer, King,
To whom the lips of children
Made sweet hosannas ring.
Thou art the King of Israel,
Thou David's royal Son,
Who in the Lord's name comest,
The King and Blessed One.

All glory, laud, and honor
To thee, Redeemer, King,
To whom the lips of children
Made sweet hosannas ring.
The company of angels
Are praising thee on high,
And mortal men and all things
Created make reply.

All glory, laud, and honor
To thee, Redeemer, King,
To whom the lips of children
Made sweet hosannas ring.
The people of the Hebrews

With psalms before thee went;
Our praise and prayer and anthems
Before thee we present.

All glory, laud, and honor
To thee, Redeemer, King,
To whom the lips of children
Made sweet hosannas ring.
To thee, before thy Passion,
They sang their hymns of praise;
To thee, now high exalted,
Our melody we raise.

All glory, laud, and honor
To thee, Redeemer, King,
To whom the lips of children
Made sweet hosannas ring.
Thou didst accept their praises;
Accept the prayers we bring,
Who in all good delightest,
Thou good and gracious King.

and brought back to life such ancient songs as "Come, O Come, Emmanuel" and "Good Christian Men, Rejoice."

One afternoon in 1851, while plowing through another dusty volume of church history, Neale came across a song written by Theodulph of Orleans. He studied the words for some time, feeling their rhythm and pacing in the original Latin before picking up a pencil and writing an English translation. Dedicated to preserving Theodulph's original intent and imagery, Neale carefully reworked his interpretation into rhymed lines.

Neale judged the music that had accompanied "All Glory, Laud, and Honor" to be unworthy of such lofty lyrics, so he matched the verses to a song that was twice their age. "Ein andachtiges Gebet" was penned in the 1600s by Melchior Teschner, a German pastor and composer who died during a Cossack invasion when he was just fifty-one. Without Neale's using his tune, Teschner, a man who gave his life for his faith, would surely be all but forgotten today, but thanks to Neale, the preacher's devotion to his Lord lives on.

Neither Neale nor Theodulph would have considered "All Glory, Laud, and Honor" a song for the Easter season, but in the late 1800s, churches began to use the hymn during Palm Sunday services. This marriage of song and day seemed natural in relation to the way Jesus was greeted as he rode into Jerusalem. At that moment, thousands lined the streets to honor the man they hoped would be their earthly ruler. Though most in that crowd soon turned their backs on Jesus, his voice was not silenced. Today, all around the world people who, like Theodulph and Neale, proclaim the Good News still follow Christ's lessons even when others try to silence them.

2

$\mathscr{A}$las! and Did My Savior Bleed (At the Cross?)

$\mathscr{O}$ne of the most powerful Christian anthems ever written was penned three centuries ago by the father of English hymns, Isaac Watts. Yet in a sense, this familiar and dynamic Easter favorite remained unfinished for more than 150 years until a veteran of the American Civil War provided an uplifting and personal spiritual coda to the original hymn's inspired verses and transformed "Alas! and Did My Savior Bleed" into "At the Cross." In the process, the song's title was not only changed, but the song itself changed from a familiar worship service closing hymn to an illustrious Easter anthem.

Few things about Isaac Watts's life were normal. On July 17, 1674, the day Isaac Watts was born, his father was confined in a dark, dank prison cell. The elder Watts had earned his sentence because of his views of Christian worship, views that did not conform to the laws and traditions of the Church of England. As church leaders soon learned, in the case of Isaac, the apple did not fall far from the tree. Even as a youth, Watts criticized the Psalms sung in Anglican worship. He labeled them as dull, convoluted, and lacking in contemporary meaning. Isaac's

father, both proud of and bemused by his son's views, challenged Isaac to do better. He urged him to create new music better reflecting of New Testament faith.

Over the next fifty years Watts met this challenge by composing more than seven hundred hymns and becoming the best-known writer of sacred songs in the world. In a sense, he revolutionized Christian music presentation, thereby opening the door to new thinking in every facet of church worship. Remarkably, Watts did not compose his songs thinking as a musician but as a Bible student. Therefore his theologically sound musical messages reached not only his generation but also each new generation of Christians, inspiring them in ways that few other songwriters ever have. In fact, even today it is hard to imagine a worship service that does not owe something to Watts.

Watts was driven as few have ever been driven to fully understand each facet of his faith. Probably because of an independent streak, as a teen, Watts refused admittance to several major English colleges including Oxford and Cambridge, instead entering an independent school at Stoke Newington. Though the obviously gifted Watts chose to receive his formal schooling at lesser-known private academies, it did not hold the lad back. As a teen Watts often spent days without sleep or physical exercise while studying the Bible as well as all the theological books he could lay his hands on. He marked those volumes, wrote notes on the sides of the pages, and composed papers with new thoughts, challenging long-accepted ideas. Before he reached his twentieth birthday, he had become one of England's most eloquent biblical scholars. At the age of twenty-four he began a career as a pastor that quickly saw him recognized as one of the most esteemed church leaders of

the Calvinist movement — this in spite of the fact that his frail health often left him bedridden for months at a time.

Because he was first a theologian, Watts viewed music in terms of biblical constraints. He framed his songs within the confines of the true nature of Christ's life on earth and his death on the cross. So when Watts took himself back in time to view the crucifixion, he so immersed himself into this study that it was as if he were seeing it with his own eyes. To achieve this perspective, Watts pored over historical documents that fully described a Roman crucifixion. What he uncovered both overwhelmed and revolted him, and as he then reread the scriptural accounts of Good Friday, he became so humbled through the realization of the suffering Jesus endured for sinners that he felt moved to write about it in graphic terms.

On that day in 1707, as Watts penned his newest hymn, he broke open a fresh way of looking at Easter. Never before had the pain of Christ's death been painted with such intense descriptive passion. It was horrifying. In the second verse of "Alas! and Did My Savior Bleed," the imagery fully reflects the writer's awe of the price paid by his Lord. In Watts's mind this was anything but a pretty picture. Perhaps that is why this verse is rarely found in hymnals today.

> Thy body slain, sweet Jesus, thine,
> And bathed in its own blood,
> While all exposed to wrath divine
> The glorious Suff'rer stood!

The other unique and explicit element of this spiritual standard that is often changed today is the line "for such a worm as I." Most people don't like to see themselves in this kind of light. Watts knew that compared to the majesty and power of

Christ, he had little more worth than a mindless creature that digs through the dirt. And yet, realizing that Jesus loved him enough to die for him made the cross not just a symbol of agonizing death but also a great symbol of hope and love.

When published in 1707, "Alas! and Did My Savior Bleed" was not a hymn confined to the Easter season. In fact it was one of the most-used songs in the hymnals of the day. For more than 170 years, at most Protestant worship services, this Watts classic was the historical equivalent of "Just As I Am." It was almost exclusively employed as an invitation call. As such, it had a profound effect on American Christian music. In fact, the power of Watts's work might best be seen in the conversion testimony of the "mother of American hymns."

In 1850, a thirty-year-old blind woman found herself at a church service. This fragile sinner had been moved by the message she had heard that day, but she didn't feel the urge to acknowledge her faith until the invitation hymn was played. When Fanny Crosby heard "Alas! and Did My Savior Bleed," she took special note of Watts's description of Christ dying on the cross. Crosby later told her friends, "When they sang the lyric, 'Here, Lord, I give myself away / 'tis all that I can do,' then I had to yield to the call. My very soul flooded with celestial light. I sprang to my feet, shouting 'Hallelujah.' "

Thanks in no small part to the dynamic message found in Watts's hymn, Fanny Crosby composed hundreds of sacred favorites, including "To God Be the Glory," "Jesus Is Tenderly Calling," "Blessed Assurance," "Rescue the Perishing," and "Tell Me the Story of Jesus." Yet it was the Watts hymn that seemed to be the model for her own Christian service.

Like Fanny Crosby, Ralph Hudson was continually drawn to "Alas! and Did My Savior Bleed." Hudson had been a Union

Alas! and Did My Savior Bleed
(At the Cross?)

Alas! and did my Savior bleed,
And did my Sov'reign die?
Would he devote that sacred head
For such a worm as I?

Thy body slain, sweet Jesus, thine,
And bathed in its own blood,
While all exposed to wrath divine
The glorious Suff'rer stood!

Was it for crimes that I had done
He groaned upon the tree?
Amazing pity, grace unknown,
And love beyond degree!

Well might the sun in darkness hide,
And shut his glories in,
When God, the mighty Maker, died
For man, the creature's sin.

Thus might I hide my blushing face
While his dear cross appears,
Dissolve my heart in thankfulness,
And melt mine eyes to tears.

But drops of grief can ne'er repay
The debt of love I owe;
Here, Lord, I give myself away,
'Tis all that I can do.

Refrain
At the cross, at the cross
Where I first saw the light,
And the burden of my heart rolled away,
It was there by faith
I received my sight,
And now I am happy all the day.

soldier in the Civil War. He served for three long years and survived some of the bloodiest battles fought to preserve the United States. He not only felt blessed to escape the war with his health, but he also felt moved to use the remainder of his life in service to the God who had seen him through those many battles. In the days after the war Hudson told his friends, "I have been saved for something." He then began looking for it.

Hudson taught music at Ohio's Mount Union College during the week and spent his weekends telling the story of God's grace in pulpits. He also found time to compose more than forty hymns. When he studied Watts's classic hymn, the music teacher felt it was not complete. It needed something more. Yes, Hudson acknowledged, Watts had written a powerful vision of the suffering of the cross, painting a haunting verbal image of the debt that all Christians owe Christ, but Hudson believed the message needed to end with the uplifting hope found in the resurrection. So, in very simple language, set to music that was much more elementary in tone and tempo than that of the original hymn, Hudson added the reason that Christians were drawn to the cross and described the hope found in Easter.

> *At the cross, at the cross*
> *Where I first saw the light,*
> *And the burden of my heart rolled away,*
> *It was there by faith*
> *I received my sight,*
> *And now I am happy all the day.*

At first glance, the chorus and verses seemingly don't go together. Yet when sung, they obviously do complement each other. The haunting melody of the verses serves to set up the triumphant response of those who find the living Christ by taking

another look at the meaning not just of Christ on the cross but of a cross that could not stop his mission or his life.

By the early 1900s, Hudson's reframe had been largely accepted as a vital part of Watts's original lyrics. With this musical marriage, "At the Cross" became one of the most beloved hymns used at Easter services around the world. Isaac Watts would have probably been one of the first to enthusiastically sing Ralph Hudson's chorus. It was his nature to look at the hopeful side of faith and celebrate words that touched the heart rather than entranced the mind. He once told a congregation that his views on spreading the message were much different than those of most pastors.

"I hate the thoughts of making anything in religion heavy or tiresome," Watts explained. "Suppose two preachers were desired to minister to the same subject. One of them has all the beauty, force, and skill of clear and calm reasoning; the other not only instructs well, but powerfully moves the affections with sacred oratory. Which of these two will best secure the attention of the people, and guard them from drowsiness or wandering? Surely, he that touches the heart will fix the eyes and the ears and all the powers; while he that merely endeavors to inform the head will find many wandering eyes, and some sleepers."

It took both Watts and Hudson to finish one of the most moving of all Easter hymns, to give it the power needed to fully touch the soul. One composer told the Easter story in stark imagery, while the other delivered the message of hope found at the cross in a language even a child could understand. Together, these two brought Christ's death and resurrection to life in a timeless manner that still leads sinners home and leaves believers awestruck.

3

*W*hen I Survey
the Wondrous Cross

*I*saac Watts is considered to be the "Father of English Hymnody." Through his body of more than seven hundred published hymns, this son of a Congregationalist minister altered the way worship services are conducted. He opened Christian music to include new, exciting songs that contain personal testimonies in carefully crafted lyrics. He thus dramatically changed not just the way people sang in church but also how they related music to their Christian faith. "When I Survey the Wondrous Cross" is often considered the greatest song this famous Englishman wrote.

Watts was born in 1674 in Southampton, England. As a child he showed unusual intellect, having mastered Latin, Greek, French, and Hebrew before reaching his teens. It also was during this time that Watts's rebellious streak began to surface. He began to critique his father's church services, telling his family bluntly that church was not inspirational for any age group. He even went so far as to explain to his father, "The singing of God's praise is the part of worship most closely related to heaven; but its performance among us is the worst on earth."

The amused elder Watts told his son that if singing from the book of Psalms was boring, then maybe Isaac should write some new hymns that were more exciting.

While most young people would have passed on the challenge, Watts accepted it and in the process revolutionized worship. But this transformation didn't happen overnight. In fact it might not have happened at all if something had not forced Watts out of what he considered his life's calling.

Based on reviews by his contemporaries, there is little doubt Watts would have become one of England's most dynamic preachers if his health had not failed him. While still in his twenties he was often so sick he was unable to keep up the daily challenges of leading a church. Thus, incapable of doing more than occasionally addressing a congregation as a guest speaker, he turned to studying and writing. In 1707, as he prepared to help lead a communion service, Watts found himself entranced by Galatians 6:14: "But God forbid that I should glory, save in the cross of our Lord Jesus Christ, by whom the world is crucified unto me, and I unto the world."

After reading this verse several times, Watts picked up a quill, dipped it in ink, and set about composing a deeply personal poem. During this period, first-person testimonies were all but unheard of; thus when Watts wrote the word "I" in that initial line, it was revolutionary. The fact that he would publish his own views of faith was all but unbelievable. Yet in 1707, Watts included his "Crucifixion to the World by the Cross of Christ" in a book called *Hymns and Spiritual Songs*. Two years later he republished the hymn but changed the second line from "Where the young Prince of Glory died" to "On which the Prince of Glory died." Also, since many who had sung his original version had been appalled by the gory nature of the

fourth stanza, Watts suggested that it could be deleted. Thus few today have ever sung:

> *His dying crimson, like a robe,*
> *Spreads o'er his body on the tree;*
> *Then am I dead to all the globe*
> *And all the globe is dead to me.*

Even with the fourth verse cut, hundreds of churches, even those who used many of Watts's other songs, refused to sing this new anthem. Christian leaders felt that the "I" made this a hymn of "human composure." To them this focus on the individual made it unfit for congregational worship because it centered on only one man's relationship with God. Yet as "When I Survey the Wondrous Cross" gained exposure, theologians discovered that most Christians desired to embrace the song because it reflected their own personal relationship with Christ. Hence, through this song, Watts opened the door for millions to have their first one-on-one connection with their Savior.

Five decades after it was written, "When I Survey the Wondrous Cross" was not only widely accepted in England but also had found favor in the United States. Yet it took another sixty years before the great hymn was given the tune most familiar to worshipers today.

Lowell Mason was a banker in Savannah, Georgia, when he came across Watts's testimony about the cross. Sensing the original tune was out of step with modern worship, Mason sought out a new score for the lyrics. While doing research into ancient church music, Mason stumbled across a Gregorian chant. In 1824, thirty-two-year-old Mason reworked that melody and fitted it to lyrics found in Watts's "When I Survey the Wondrous Cross." He then taught the new arrangement to the

When I Survey the Wondrous Cross

When I survey the wondrous cross
where the young Prince of Glory died,
my richest gain I count but loss,
and pour contempt on all my pride.

Forbid it, Lord, that I should boast,
save in the cross of Christ, my God:
all the vain things that charm me most,
I sacrifice them to his blood.

See, from his head, his hands, his feet,
sorrow and love flow mingled down!
Did e'er such love and sorrow meet,
or thorns compose so rich a crown?

Were the whole realm of nature mine,
that were an offering far too small;
love so amazing, so divine,
demands my soul, my life, my all.

choir at the First Independent Presbyterian Church of Savannah. The hymn was so well received at that first Sunday performance that it quickly found a publisher. This is the version now most commonly heard throughout the world.

Mason moved back to Boston a few years later and became one of the most respected hymn composers and publishers of his time. Certainly Christian music is much richer thanks to this man, but his impact on worship is minor compared to Isaac Watts's.

Watts dramatically changed worship by giving it a vitality and personal quality it had never known. His hymns were triumphant statements of faith that brought the New Testament alive in music. His music made the worshiper not a spectator but a participant in the sharing of the gospel. Because he had the courage to challenge convention, he was likely responsible for millions hearing the call of the Lord in songs as well as in sermons. Without Watts's leading the way, there would have been no great hymns written by the likes of Charles Wesley, John Newton, or James Montgomery. In the light of his incredible contributions, most feel Watts's greatest work was his "When I Survey the Wondrous Cross."

Charles Wesley penned more than seven thousand hymns, and many of these are still being used by churches all over the globe. Yet Wesley was so awed by Isaac Watts's Easter anthem that he said he would give up all of his hymns just to have written "When I Survey the Wondrous Cross." Certainly few writers have ever captured the full impact of the cross on an individual's salvation as did Watts when he penned this magnificent hymn.

The History of Lent

*T*here is no date designated for the beginning of the observance of what is now known as Lent. Nevertheless, references in several different historical texts reveal that this tradition connected to the Easter season goes back to at least the second century. In fact, some scholars believe the crucifixion and resurrection may have been formally marked and celebrated by the apostles and their early followers in Lenten-type worship rituals. If this is the case, then Lent took root in the years just after the first Easter.

Irenaeus seems to verify this early beginning for Lent in a letter to Pope Victor I in the late second century. Irenaeus wrote that he had witnessed Christians from different areas celebrating the resurrection of Christ in a wide variety of ways, observing, "Some think that they ought to fast for one day, some for two, others for still more; some make their 'day' last forty hours on end. Such variation in the observance did not originate in our own day, but very much earlier, in the time of our forefathers."

This report clearly suggests the observance of Easter was long established by the year 200, and an early form of Lent was also already being practiced. That many church leaders of the period called the twelve disciples "the forefathers" indicates

this practice had a solid link to the actual beginnings of Christianity. Thus this custom predates any official church ruling on the subject by at least two centuries.

Even during the initial observance of the time leading up to Easter, the church had already embraced a threefold purpose for the observation. The first came from the early church custom of baptizing new converts on the anniversary of Christ's resurrection. These converts were to set aside time leading up to Easter to study what it meant to be a Christian. The classes taught by church leaders were very serious and the instruction much more detailed than that taught in most modern congregations. The second element of preparing for Easter focused on Christians turning inward and looking at their own shortcomings. This self-judgment was a part of searching for ways to put sin behind them and better emulate the Lord in their personal and public lives.

The final element of the annual observance dealt with finding the lost sheep and convincing them to come back to the flock. Church members sought out those who had strayed from their congregations and offered them the chance to once again be a part of a Christian fellowship.

While the threefold worship focus of the period leading up to Easter was fairly consistent throughout the early Christian world, the time these observances took place and their length still varied widely from region to region. Church leadership recognized this issue and felt the practice would have more meaning if it were uniformly observed and practiced. But because Christianity was still not considered a legal religion, they were powerless to even offer suggestions. In 313, when Christianity became the official religion of the Roman Empire, church leaders decided that standards of worship practices should be put in place.

The 325 Council of Nicaea is best remembered for establishing official dates to observe both Christmas and Easter. At the same time the council also established rules for the observance of the weeks leading up to Easter. The council's decrees emphasized a forty-day period of fasting. This forty-day period was likely chosen because of the significance of the number forty in both Christ's life and biblical history. Forty was the number of days Christ fasted during his temptation by Satan in the wilderness. Moses had observed forty days of fasting and praying during the time he was given the Ten Commandments. Elijah once fasted for forty days and forty nights, and Noah watched it rain for the same period of time. The people of Israel wandered for forty years in the wilderness. So the early church considered forty a sacred number and therefore considered it worthy of being employed as the countdown to the holiest of holidays. Still, even with the forty days in place and a time set aside for Easter, church leaders were constantly bombarded with questions about the specifics of the observance. The most common problems dealt with what could be eaten and what the Christian definition of fasting was. After about a century of various churches' applying different rules to the forty days leading up to Easter, the church hierarchy more fully defined how this period of time was to be observed.

Their first edict concerned the actual forty days. They decided that each Sunday should be a time of celebration and feasting. As this day was set aside to glorify God, it would not be included in the forty days of fasting. Further refinements led to the holiday beginning on a Wednesday rather than on a Monday, making the period of fasting and worship exactly forty days when Sundays were excluded. The day beginning the season of remembrance and dedication was to be called

Ash Wednesday. As complicated as the formula for determining when Easter falls each year is, this system has remained in place for fifteen centuries.

Next the church leaders tackled the rules of fasting. They initially decided that no one could consume any meat or animal products during the forty days. This meant that eggs and milk were also on the forbidden food list. The one meal allowed each day would be held at three in the afternoon. Church members were admonished to adhere to this edict as a way of showing a small bit of sacrifice to honor a Savior who had given everything for them. Except for a few minor changes, these rules were accepted and adhered to for several hundred years.

In the late sixth century, Pope Gregory finally gave the forty days of fasting and remembrance a name. It is thought he titled this time "Lent" because of the Anglo-Saxon word *leneten*, meaning "spring" or the time when the year lengthens. This seemed to naturally tie in with the period of the year when Easter was celebrated. While Gregory would have been familiar with this Anglo-Saxon term, he might have also taken the name Lent from other languages of the period that had similar words meaning "to fast." Either way, more than five centuries after the tradition began, Gregory finally gave it a name. Over time, other facets of Lent were also given specific titles.

The first Sunday of Lent became Passion Sunday, and the last Sunday was officially designated as Palm Sunday. The week leading up to Easter was named the Passion Tide, or as it is now known, Holy Week. The day Christ served the Passover meal or the Last Supper was called Maundy Thursday. The word *Maundy* comes from the Latin for "command" (*mandatum*). It refers to the command Jesus gave at the Last Supper that his disciples should love one another. The day he was crucified

was designated as God's Friday, which has become Good Friday. Finally, the Saturday of Passion Tide, characterized by preparation for the moment when Christ rises from the dead, was called Holy Saturday.

Over time churches added customs to the observance of specific days. One of the most meaningful was the removal of all flowers and decorative elements from sanctuaries on Good Friday. On this day only a few candles or lamps would be lit in order to keep the mood somber and dark. Clergy felt this environment created an atmosphere enabling worshipers to fully understand the importance of Christ being nailed to the cross.

Another tradition sprang forth on Easter Sunday. On this day of hope the church was brightened up to enhance the celebration of the resurrection. Many sanctuaries were decorated with dogwood blossoms and lilies. Legend has it the dogwood was used for Christ's cross. Since the crucifixion, the tree's white, cross-shaped blossoms have been said to reflect the Savior's purity, while the red highlights in the middle of the flowers stand for his blood. Early Christians believed dogwood trees flowered during the season of Lent as a reminder of the power and glory of Jesus Christ. The lily was the most prized bloom of the spring season. In some places lilies were also a symbol of royalty. Thus remembering God's Son with this flower both offered honor and showed great respect.

Until the Reformation, Lent was recognized and observed by all churches. When Martin Luther broke away from the Catholic Church, many traditions and sacraments were discarded by various splinter groups. While Luther was at the forefront of much of this change, he was not responsible for many Protestant groups' discarding Lent. In fact, he wrote, "Lent, Palm Sunday, and the Holy Week shall be retained, not

to force anyone to fast, but to preserve the Passion history and the Gospels appointed for that season."

While many traditional Protestant churches kept Lent and continued to observe it, others not only tossed Lent from their worship customs, but they also did away with Christmas and Easter services. Thus for many Christians the practices observed during the forty days of Lent became more and more obscure.

Today, while it is practiced much differently than it was eighteen hundred years ago, Lent is an important facet of the Easter season for hundreds of millions around the globe. Many denominations can even claim an unbroken line of observing Lent going back almost to the time of Christ. Many other Christian groups that for centuries ignored the forty-day period leading up to Easter now recognize the historical significance of Lent and are incorporating certain facets of the tradition into their Easter customs. More so than at any time in the past five centuries, Lent appears to be gaining popularity and acceptance.

Since its beginnings, Lent has been a time to reconsider individual faith, to rededicate oneself to that faith, and to be thankful for the gift of eternal life given on the first Easter. Therefore, no matter the extent to which Lent is embraced in individual congregations, the goal of this season is one that should be a part of every Christian's preparation for Easter.

5

Christ the Lord
Is Risen Today

It is hard to picture an Easter service without the powerful and uplifting strains of "Christ the Lord Is Risen Today," but in colonial America, most churches did not sing songs that proclaimed Christ, his birth, his life, or his resurrection. In fact, rather than being uplifting, most musical services were unspirited and somber. In most minds, the musical facet of worship was to be endured, not enjoyed.

Until three centuries ago, music in a majority of Protestant churches came only from the book of Psalms. These scriptural offerings were set to just a handful of tunes. A congregation might well have sung three different psalms in one service, all to the same melody. In this system there were no melodic personal testimonies, no songs of grace, and no mention of Jesus. From a musical standpoint, worship essentially stopped around the time David lived.

As a teen, pioneering English preacher and songwriter Isaac Watts saw a need for a musical revolution. He wanted to change the spirit of worship, to energize it. He felt one of the ways to make that shift was through music. Others including Charles Wesley soon followed, bringing the New Testament into worship

service music and revitalizing the church experience for millions. But, as is often the case with change, the established church did not make this step an easy one. In fact, it took a different stage than the Anglican Church for Wesley's worship to be initially accepted.

Wesley, "the sweet singer of Methodism," was born in Epworth, Lincolnshire, England, on December 18, 1707. He was the youngest son of a preacher and from his childhood seemed destined for the pulpit. In 1726, to prepare for the pastorate, he entered Christ Church College, Oxford. There, revealing a bit of the rebellious nature that would fuel his passionate Christian faith, he formed the Holy Club, a group dedicated to a methodical approach to Bible study. This rather informal organization became the foundation of the Methodist movement and eventually split off from the established Church of England.

Ordained an Anglican priest in 1735, Charles did not immediately begin his Christian service. Instead of seeking a church appointment in the British Isles, he sought adventure, joining his brother John in sailing to the New World colony of Georgia. In America, Charles found work with the British governor and, in his spare time, got to know the country and its settlers. Though he loved the rough and tumble world he found in Georgia, health problems forced Charles to sail back to England just a year after his arrival in America. His farewell vow to his New World friends that he would return to America as a missionary was never realized. As it turned out, God had other things in mind for the young man.

Because he had seen America, Charles became a celebrity in England. He was invited to numerous important social galas, was a popular dinner guest of the most elite British families, and was even granted a royal audience. Yet this fame offered little

solace to a man who had a strong desire to change the world. In fact, even as people lined up to hear him speak of the New World, he grew deeply depressed. Now thirty-one, he felt that life was passing him by. But just as illness had brought him back to England, illness finally brought his destiny into clear focus.

In May 1738, Charles grew suddenly sick. He was so weak that those close to him thought he would die. A group of Moravians in Little Britain, not far from St. Paul's Cathedral, offered him their home for recovery. These dedicated Christians might have been considered extremists by the Church of England, but Charles was deeply moved by the humble concern and gracious charity of his hosts. Their lack of concern about social status and their desire to help the poor and lost seemed to mirror Christ. Observing this display of faith rekindled a passion in Charles he had not known since his first days of college. As he observed these men's love for God shown in their words and actions, his soul was set aflame and his physical strength returned. In an instant he felt a strong call not only to serve God but also to write music that reflected this new passion for preaching the gospel. On May 24, an inspired Wesley composed the first of more than three thousand hymns.

> *Where shall my wondering soul begin?*
> *How shall I all to heaven aspire?*
> *A slave redeemed from death and sin,*
> *A brand plucked from eternal fire!*
> *How shall I equal triumphs raise*
> *Or sing my great Deliverer's praise?*

Less than a year later, Wesley was traveling across England preaching in scores of different revival-type settings. Though the Anglican Church considered his style too evangelical for

their churches, thousands flocked to hear Charles and his brother John preach in open fields and modest, nondenominational sanctuaries. And what moved the crowds as much as the men's sermons were Charles's new hymns. Songs such as "Oh for a Thousand Tongues to Sing" brought worship to life and joy to the hearts of men and women who had never sung songs of New Testament praise. Seeing the impact his music was making spurred Charles to step up his writing. For the remainder of his life he composed at a rate of almost a song a day. Few men have ever been this driven or been given so many messages to share. Revolutionaries often have great energy to go with their huge passion, and this was surely true of Wesley.

Charles was not just a student of the Bible; he was a man with a deep thirst to learn. His intellectual journeys often took him in a host of different literary directions. He studied theology and music at the same time, and some of the inspiration for both his sermons and his song lyrics came from old musical books of the Catholic Church. Though there were several publications of the period containing English translations of early Latin hymns, Wesley discovered the foundation for his greatest Easter hymn in *Lyra Davidica*. In this book of forgotten hymns of the Middle Ages, Charles was moved by a work called "Jesus Christ Is Risen Today."

> *Jesus Christ is risen today, Halle-halle-lujah.*
> *Our triumphant holy day,*
> *Who so lately on the cross*
> *Suffered to redeem our loss.*
> *Haste ye females from your fright,*
> *Take to Galilee your flight;*
> *To his sad disciples say,*

Christ the Lord Is Risen Today

Christ the Lord is risen today, Alleluia!
Sons of men and angels say, Alleluia!
Raise your joys and triumphs high,
  Alleluia!
Sing, ye heavens, and earth, reply,
  Alleluia!

Love's redeeming work is done, Alleluia!
Fought the fight, the battle won, Alleluia!
Lo! the Sun's eclipse is over, Alleluia!
Lo! He sets in blood no more, Alleluia!

Vain the stone, the watch, the seal,
  Alleluia!
Christ hath burst the gates of hell,
  Alleluia!
Death in vain forbids his rise, Alleluia!
Christ hath opened paradise, Alleluia!

Lives again our glorious King, Alleluia!
Where, O death, is now thy sting?
  Alleluia!
Once he died our souls to save, Alleluia!
Where thy victory, O grave? Alleluia!

Soar we now where Christ hath led,
  Alleluia!
Following our exalted head, Alleluia!
Made like him, like him we rise, Alleluia!

Ours the cross, the grave, the skies,
  Alleluia!

Hail, the Lord of earth and heaven,
  Alleluia!
Praise to thee by both be given, Alleluia!
Thee we greet triumphant now, Alleluia!
Hail, the resurrection, thou, Alleluia!

King of glory, Soul of bliss, Alleluia!
Everlasting life is this, Alleluia!
Thee to know, Thy power to prove,
  Alleluia!
Thus to sing and thus to love, Alleluia!

Hymns of praise then let us sing, Alleluia!
Unto Christ, our heavenly King, Alleluia!
Who endured the cross and grave,
  Alleluia!
Sinners to redeem and save. Alleluia!

But the pains that he endured, Alleluia!
Our salvation have procured, Alleluia!
Now above the sky he's King, Alleluia!
Where the angels ever sing. Alleluia!

Jesus Christ is risen today, Alleluia!
Our triumphant holy day, Alleluia!
Who did once upon the cross, Alleluia!
Suffer to redeem our loss. Alleluia!

Jesus Christ is risen today.
In our Paschal joy and feast
Let the Lord of life be blest;
Let the Holy Trine be praised,
And thankful hearts to heaven be raised.

Though Charles was intrigued by the old hymn and its message, he felt it was not suited for his evangelistic-style meetings. Rather than set the hymn aside, he used the old song's theme as an outline for his own views of the resurrection. In short order, Wesley created a new hymn called "Christ the Lord Is Risen Today." But rather than immediately debut it, as he did most of his songs, he decided to hold this hymn for an upcoming event, one he felt was the most important of his life.

Because the Church of England would not accept their worship methods, the Wesleys decided to create a new church in London. They bought a deserted iron foundry and remodeled it into a decidedly different house of worship. When The Foundry Meeting House was dedicated in 1739, the first song sung in this revolutionary hall was the one Charles had saved for the occasion, "Christ the Lord Is Risen Today." As he looked out at the hundreds singing his song of resurrection, Charles knew these Christians felt the true joy of worshiping a living Savior. This is what Watts had wanted when he first went to work on creating modern hymns and what Wesley's church was realizing in the old iron factory. For Charles it was an answered prayer.

Later that year, the dedication song, along with several other Wesley originals, was published in Charles's first book of songs, *The Foundry Collection*. In the hymnal, "Christ the Lord Is Risen Today" was designated as the Easter hymn. Wesley published the song with simple four-line stanzas and, as originally composed,

the hymn did not contain the now familiar "alleluia" at the end of each line. That exclamation, an ancient Hebrew expression of praise, was added later by an unknown hymnal editor who must have felt those singing this powerful song should shout out their joy that Christ was alive. The addition caught on, and over the course of the next few decades, "Christ the Lord Is Risen Today" was usually sung with either "hallelujah" or "alleluia," depending upon the hymnal being used. Today the "alleluia" is the most familiar addition to Wesley's joyful lyrics.

Though still one of the most important songs of the Easter season, the original exuberant effect created by the singing of this song has been somewhat tempered, if not fully lost. To completely comprehend the dynamics of what "Christ the Lord Is Risen Today" meant to Christians in churches in England and America around the time of the American Revolution, the song must be viewed through the eyes of those worshipers. For those Christians, church music was no longer locked into the era of David. Thanks to revolutionaries such as Watts and Wesley, hymns brought the events of the cross, the tomb, and the resurrection to life in a way that moved believers to tears at the same time their voices sang out the good news. Modern Christians can fully understand this only when they imagine the joy and zealous spirit that could be found when singing about Christ's resurrection for the very first time.

Along with a few others, this Charles Wesley song was a part of a movement that changed worship forever by capturing the uplifting nature of Christian faith. It brought hope to the heart and meaning to the season. Therefore Easter was not just greatly impacted by "Christ the Lord Is Risen Today," but so was the manner in which Christians proclaim the victory found in this glorious day.

Were You There

*E*aster is about freedom. Every Christian knows that what Christ offered us through his death and resurrection was freedom from the grave. Yet there is also another more immediate freedom that comes with accepting Jesus as Savior, a freedom felt when all sins are forgiven. This is a freedom that allows us to take wing and soar with a new purpose in our lives. Suddenly there are no boundaries or restraints, and our talents can finally be fully realized. But does this freedom brought by salvation apply to someone who is in chains and has no hope of being freed? Can Easter really mean anything to a slave?

The answer is obvious and can be found in the spiritual music of American slaves. To these oppressed people, faith offered something much deeper and more meaningful than just forgiveness of sins; it provided freedom from bondage. While thankfully slavery is now a dark relic of American history, the slaves' spirituals are joyfully alive to this day.

The great musical traditions of the native tribes along Africa's west coast were among the few things that slave traders

couldn't steal from their captives. The captured Africans took the beat, the harmonies, and the unique lead vocals to America, where they passed their songs from generation to generation as a way of connecting with a place that had allowed their bodies and spirits to run free.

The music of Africa and the message of salvation first came together in the areas around Savannah, Georgia. There, on huge rice and cotton plantations, the sounds of men and women harmonizing in the fields brought an ironically peaceful atmosphere to an institution awash in sin. While the choral-like music might have signaled a sense of peace and contentment, the subjects the slave writers chose as the themes of their songs painted the true story of oppression.

The spiritual feel of *gulla* (African folk music) had been in place for hundreds of years. Yet as the masters' traditions and beliefs became a part of the slaves' lives, the message of the songs changed. Through hearing Bible stories, slaves began to understand there were two kinds of bondage; one was physical and the other spiritual. Because there was so little they could do about unchaining their bodies, these men and women vigorously sought freedom for their souls.

The Bible is filled with stories of God relating to slaves. Christ himself taught that all of us are slaves to something. Thus, accepting Christ and fully embracing his message was usually easier for the slave than it was for the master. Ironically, in these times in the Old South, the pupils often became the teachers. Many times it was the field workers or house servants — men and women who had no earthly possessions, no legal rights, and no social standing — who provided the model for Christian charity. They freely shared what little they had,

took care of the sick, and even prayed for their owners. For many the blight of slavery was first brought into sharp focus through the pure and undefiled faith shown in the spiritual lives of American slaves.

One of the ways these oppressed people spread the hope of a better life and the joy of salvation was by taking their traditional music and adapting set Christian themes to it. Using the stories of Adam, Noah, Jonah, Elijah, and scores of other biblical figures, African Americans created songs explaining these ancient experiences in ways everyone could understand. As you listen to "Joshua Fit the Battle" or "Swing Low, Sweet Chariot," you not only hear the story but see and feel it too. It is as if you have been transported by the music to the day and place of the actual events. Although musically untrained, these composers and their choirs gave birth to the greatest American music of that time.

Many of the spirituals that have survived to this day embrace the joy of being saved. The harmonies, the rhythms, and the phrasing naturally create excitement. These songs rapidly move the heart, mind, and body. Hands can't keep from clapping, feet can't keep from dancing, and voices can't keep from singing and shouting. But not all spirituals were upbeat and exuberant. Some reflected not only the trials of a Christian life but also the pain of slavery. It was one of these seemingly downbeat songs that first found favor with the established church audience and dramatically changed the way millions looked at Christ's crucifixion.

"Were You There" moves the soul by asking haunting and personal questions of those who stood by and allowed God's Son to be executed. This song puts each Christian on the witness

Were You There

Were you there when they crucified my Lord?
Were you there when they crucified my Lord?
O! Sometimes it causes me to tremble, tremble, tremble!
Were you there when they crucified my Lord?

Were you there when they nailed him to the tree?
Were you there when they nailed him to the tree?
O! Sometimes it causes me to tremble, tremble, tremble!
Were you there when they nailed him to the tree?

Were you there when they laid him in the tomb?
Were you there when they laid him in the tomb?
O! Sometimes it causes me to tremble, tremble, tremble!
Were you there when they laid him in the tomb?

Were you there when he rose up from the dead?
Were you there when he rose up from the dead?
O! Sometimes it causes me to tremble, tremble, tremble!
Were you there when he rose up from the dead?

stand and asks questions most do not want to answer. Through the lyrics of "Were You There," the unknown writer paints a picture with very simple and direct imagery. In each succeeding verse, the sights, sounds, and reality of the crucifixion are chillingly portrayed. As much as any other song about the cross and the day Christ died, "Were You There" creates a picture that lingers long after the final note and words have drifted away. This spiritual haunts many who sing it.

There is a personal element in this song rarely found in other Easter anthems. There is a theme of regret and guilt that echoes in the line "sometimes it causes me to tremble." This type of fear — the fear brought on by having caused a man's death — was familiar to the American slave. They had seen horrible punishment firsthand. They had known brutality. Like Christ, many of them had been brutally whipped. So the slave — unlike most Christians of that time — could relate to the events leading to Christ's death. The writer of this song could easily feel the humiliation, the suffering, and the pain Jesus felt the day he was judged and executed.

By the late 1800s, "Were You There" made its way out of the slave fields and small black churches and into mainstream worship services of white congregations. The arrangement, the pacing, and the tune were changed very little. The feel of the *gulla* music remained intact. When a white congregation sang "Were You There" for the first time, an important message was subtly passed along to all Christians: while the color of skin may vary from person to person, the color of a soul is the same. Thus, contrary to the thinking of some whites of that era, even uneducated slaves were worthy of salvation and, no less, of respect. Therefore their experience should be a testimony for

everyone, no matter what his or her background, social standing, race, or age might be. Easter was not for just one group of people; it was for everyone.

Decades before the nation began to integrate churches and schools, spirituals like "Were You There" opened the country's doors to the black religious experience. These songs inspired writers of all colors to create new music that was personal, emotional, and dramatic. In fact, spirituals were the foundation of one of America's greatest exports to the world: gospel music.

It is a shame that a face and a name cannot be put to such an important, groundbreaking song. Yet maybe the fact that spirituals were the joint cries and shouts of Christians looking for the freedom that only God could bring gives the message of this song much more impact. None of us were there in body when Christ died, but all of us need to go there in spirit. To understand the gift of salvation, each sinner must realize that he or she is a slave to the world; only then does seeing Christ on the cross make the impact all the more real. Each Easter the slave song "Were You There" puts us all on the same level, reveals the guilt we all must share, and points the way to spiritual freedom. And thoughts of all of those things should make us tremble.

*J*esus Paid It All

*T*he year 1865 was pivotal in the history of the United States. The Union had been preserved by the North's victory in the Civil War, but thousands of men and a revered leader had lost their lives in the four horrific years of fighting. Never had so many given so much on American soil. So, even as peace was celebrated, the haunting cost of that peace hovered over the nation like a foreboding cloud.

Elvina Hall was well aware of the nation's gloomy mood. Even as the housewife watched the parades of troops honored as they returned home to Baltimore and their "normal lives," Hall's mind always returned to the men she knew who would never be coming home, the ones buried in distant places. Those men had parents, many had wives and children too, and the holes left by their sacrifice could never be filled.

Hall was not alone. Editorials appearing in newspapers, sermons given in churches, and prayers spoken at family tables all centered on the incredible sacrifice this war had required. It would take an entire generation for America to even begin to comprehend and put into perspective the real cost of the Civil War. Yet before that happened, Hall touched a universal chord that brought understanding, direction, and hope to millions.

Elvina Hall was forty years old when the war ended. She didn't have any children of her own but felt like all of the young people who attended Baltimore's Monument Street Methodist Church were hers. She watched them grow up, taught them in Sunday school, and listened as they shared their dreams. Each time one died in war, it broke her heart. She vowed they would never be forgotten, but she had no idea the pain she felt from the loss of these young men would spark an unforgettable song that put the death of Jesus Christ into sharp focus.

On a Sunday morning in 1865, Hall was sitting in her usual spot in the choir loft as her pastor launched into his sermon. The message that day centered on Isaiah 1:18: "Come now, and let us reason together, saith the Lord: though your sins be as scarlet, they shall be as white as snow; though they be red like crimson, they shall be as wool." Hall noted the verse but heard little of the Reverend George Schrick's words. Her mind was drifting. She was mentally going over errands that needed to be done, things she had to complete before her Sunday dinner could be served, and plans for the next week. For reasons she did not understand, she could not sit still. As her mind whirled, her hands fiddled with the *New Lute of Zion* hymnal that sat in her lap. She remained nervous and completely lost in thought, her mind miles away, until the pastor called for prayer.

Reverend Schrick's prayer that day was lengthy even by his standards. To Hall, who was so eager to accomplish her long list of chores, it seemed to go on forever. Unable to concentrate, she opened her eyes and looked out at the congregation, noting the empty places where young men had once sat, the dead boys she would never again see. Moved again by the sacrifice of the men in uniform, her mind drifted farther from the preacher's words, but now instead of considering all she needed to do, she

found herself focusing on the price Christ had paid for her salvation. Stark images of the cross and Jesus' sacrifice, the horror and the pain that were a part of that moment in history, flooded her mind. Though she was a devout Christian since childhood, at that moment the now middle-aged woman fully understood just how much she owed Jesus.

Overcome with the need to write down her thoughts, Hall felt she couldn't wait until the prayer ended. She knew that if she didn't jot them down instantly, she would lose these inspired words forever. Taking a pencil from her handbag, she quickly searched for something to write on. When she found no paper in her purse and saw none in the choir loft, her natural impulse was to give up, but the drive to write was simply too strong to dismiss. So Hall did something she constantly told children in her Sunday school classes to never do; she picked up her hymnal and opened it to the flyleaf. There she began a poem that would touch millions.

The words she jotted down that Sunday morning spewed forth so fast she could scarcely keep up. The scratch of the pencil caused several around her to lift their heads and open their eyes to see what she was doing. Hall never noticed the attention she was drawing, and even after the prayer had ended she continued to write. The congregation soon noted Hall's actions. Even her choir director, John T. Grape, saw the woman scribbling on the book in her lap. The church members wondered what the usually well-mannered Elvina was doing. It seemed so out of character for her to act in this fashion.

At the conclusion of the service, Hall picked up her hymnal and approached Reverend Schrick. Her resolute stride indicated she was on a mission. Initially she probably apologized for not paying attention to the message and then added another

Jesus Paid It All

I hear the Savior say,
"Thy strength indeed is small;
Child of weakness, watch and pray,
Find in me thine all in all."

For nothing good have I
Whereby thy grace to claim,
I'll wash my garments white
In the blood of Calvary's Lamb.

And now complete in him
My robe his righteousness,
Close sheltered 'neath his side,
I am divinely blest.

Lord, now indeed I find
Thy power and thine alone,
Can change the leper's spots
And melt the heart of stone.

When from my dying bed
My ransomed soul shall rise,
"Jesus died my soul to save,"
Shall rend the vaulted skies.

And when before the throne
I stand in him complete,
I'll lay my trophies down
All down at Jesus' feet.

Refrain
Jesus paid it all,
All to him I owe;
Sin had left a crimson stain,
He washed it white as snow.

apology for using the church's songbook for her notepad. She also probably explained that she had to write the poem; it was something God had given to her. As the preacher read over the words on the flyleaf, he sensed Hall had accomplished in a few short verses what he had not been able to do in an hour-long sermon. She had put into clear, precise words the enormity of Christ's sacrifice on the cross and the debt every person owes because of that sacrifice. Hall also composed it with a clarity that anyone could understand.

Schrick immediately took the poem to his choir director and explained the power he found in Hall's words. As the musician read over the text, he was amazed to discover the woman's verses perfectly matched a song he had already written and published called "All to Christ I Owe." Grape had never been satisfied with the lyrics in that first published work, but in Hall's words he now felt he had found the key to completing his own composition.

A few weeks later, "Jesus Paid It All" made its debut in the Monument Street Methodist Church. As the congregation listened to the words and music and considered the sacrifice of Christ, as well as the price paid by thousands for freedom in their own land, many were moved to tears. These men and women might have been the first to be deeply touched by Hall and Grape's work, but they would not be the last. Three years later the hymn was published in a book entitled *Sabbath Chords*. Within a decade it found its way into scores of other hymnals and was well known in the United States and throughout Europe. Within forty years, millions were singing it each week all around the globe.

Initially the song Elvina Hall and John Grape penned was used mainly as an invitation call. Countless churches still employ the

hymn in this way. Yet because of the imagery and the emotion found in Hall's words, "Jesus Paid It All" has also become one of the best-known Easter anthems. It has anchored cantatas and musicals and is often sung at sunrise services. Inspired by a Bible verse and by the pain and loss of war, "Jesus Paid It All" has become a definitive standard in explaining not only what was lost at the cross but also what was gained because of it.

The History of
Passion Plays

I n the Dark Ages, churches would often put on dramas. These simple plays consisted of members of the congregation, often children, acting out different biblical stories. They used various props, such as an evergreen with fruit tied to the limbs standing in for the Tree of Knowledge in the garden of Eden or a homemade cross to be used in the telling of the crucifixion story. These early pageants were the humble beginnings of what would become passion plays.

As churches grew larger, the clergy sensed a need to expand the dramas as well. During the Easter season many churches set out stations of the cross displays to present the story of the crucifixion. This drama did not use live actors but depended upon static displays to present the first Easter, and it required the audience to move or march from one set to another.

In the tenth century, a monk named Benedictines of St. Gall took the process a step farther by adding music to church dramas. Called tropes, these productions were widely accepted and were used in many church holiday celebrations. Naturally there was one that centered on the events of the first Easter.

Tropes were always presented in Latin and stuck very closely to the story of the crucifixion found in Matthew, Mark, Luke, and John.

Over the next few centuries Easter dramas grew beyond the walls of the church and into the centers of communities. Though local church leaders attempted to reign over these ever-expanding presentations, in many cases they found themselves overruled by various scholars and actors. Because of these outside influences, Easter scripts began to depart from the strict biblical stories and to embrace many of the era's dramatic influences. Latin was dismissed from the scripts, and local languages were added. New characters were written into the stories, lines that had never been recorded in the gospel became part of the scripts, and, in some cases, humor was even inserted into the final product. The resulting productions often strayed so far from the gospel that they flew in the face of church doctrine. Because many Christians were now being shown a largely fictional account of the crucifixion story, most church leaders sought to ban all Easter plays.

As with so many of the great holiday customs, Germany kept alive the tradition of Easter drama. In the fifteenth century, German actors told the Easter story in a play that had them moving through town as the audience followed along behind. Thus, the stations of the cross parades took a dramatic leap forward. But as with most forms of entertainment, its popularity could not be permanently sustained. Yet just as this type of drama began to lose its appeal, a new way to tell the old story was created.

In Germany, Spain, and France, troupes of actors came together to present what became known as passion productions. Combining many elements of religious drama from the past, these presentations were serious attempts to convey the

full range of the first Easter in a dramatic setting. Taken from the Latin word *passio*, which means suffering, these passion plays were both gritty and realistic. They pulled no punches, showing audiences the full measure of pain and tribulation that Christ endured as he was judged, ridiculed, beaten, and crucified. As most church services were conducted in Latin, and as few common people understood the language, these passion plays were often the first time many Christians fully understood what happened during the first Easter.

This was a period in history when each European community wanted to outdo the next community in every facet of life. Each city wanted to be seen as the cultural center of the area. Thus massive building projects were undertaken to construct palaces, cathedrals, and theaters. Public festivals were held to show off the new buildings. As a part of the spring celebrations, many cities put on lavish passion plays. Because of the capital set aside for them, the production values of these plays far exceeded anything that had been attempted in the past. Using dramatic costumes, huge sets, and the best-known actors in the area, these dramas not only told the story of the first Easter, but they took it to new heights in realism. The effort to make Christ's suffering and death appear real often left audiences in tears. Never before had men, women, and children come as close to understanding what Jesus did for them so long ago in Jerusalem.

In 1633, as Europe was in the midst of the bubonic plague, the city fathers of Oberammergau, Germany, came together for prayer. They promised God that if the plague deaths would cease in their community, they would produce the greatest passion play ever staged. They vowed to continue to present these plays every decade and spare no expense on sets, costumes, or promotion. After this vow, no more residents died of the plague,

and a tradition began that continues to this day. Every ten years a passion play is produced in Oberammergau that demands effort from the city's entire population. Just as they did three centuries ago, the citizens continue to come together in putting on a play that lasts eight hours.

Though some European cities continued to cling to the passion play tradition, by the end of the seventeenth century these presentations were often transformed into other types of less elaborate productions. One of the principle reasons for this was the *Messiah*. When Handel composed this oratorio, he created a new form of telling spiritual stories. As a result, churches turned their attention to choral programs rather than to passion plays as the best way to inspire Easter audiences.

Easter musicals were not the only things that diminished the popularity of passion plays. Just as important was that more and more people now had access to Bibles written in a language they could read. Thus, most could study the final days of Christ's life in the privacy of their own homes. They felt they knew the story well enough that they no longer needed to see it play out before their eyes. Another factor in the downturn of passion plays was that as easy methods of travel became more common, tastes grew more refined. When people saw plays in large cities, they often found amateur productions lacking. This was true of both small-town theater and local church dramas.

In spite of two hundred years of fading interest, the old passion play tradition did not completely die. Even in the early twentieth century a few cities in both Europe and America continued to annually stage the dramas at Easter. Still, these productions were not very well known. By 1950, few in the United States even knew what a passion play was, and outside of the Bible Belt, only a handful were performed.

The information age would have seemed a strange time for a renaissance in the production of passion plays. Yet in the twenty-first century that is just what has happened. A great deal of the biblical drama's return to the spotlight can be attributed to an independent Hollywood film. In 2004, actor-producer Mel Gibson spent millions of dollars to create a film version of the passion play. Gibson's *The Passion of the Christ* went back to the play's original concept, taking the script directly from the four gospels of the New Testament and including the graphic horror that was a very real part of the judgment of Christ and his crucifixion. What resulted was a passion play like none other. As one of the top grossing films in history, it has been viewed by hundreds of millions all around the globe. *The Passion of the Christ* sparked a renewed interest in reviving live passion plays. All over the world these dramas are once again bringing illumination to the Easter story. And because the movie stayed true to the biblical story, so do most of these new productions.

It is sad that to many the Bible is void of deep emotion. For some, the events in the four gospels contain very little passion. Yet as was discovered almost a thousand years ago, when the Word is turned into visual drama, it can be moving, touching, and have great impact. In dramatic presentations, the senses are often challenged, and the heart is deeply moved. So for many it is still true that the story of Jesus' final days on earth becomes more profound and meaningful when watched. Thus, this ancient art form, one of the oldest traditions of Easter, is as alive today as it was in the Middle Ages. As clergy realized a millennium ago, drama evokes passion in a way that few other things can.

9

Near the Cross

anny Crosby stands alone as the greatest American hymn writer and is one of the most remarkable icons in Christian music history. Not only did she write more than nine thousand different sets of lyrics, but hundreds of her religious songs were published and many remain as popular today as when they were written more than a century ago. A large part of the continued popularity of Crosby's hymns can be tied to her vision. The writer saw situations in vivid detail and was able to paint these scenes in words that brought biblical events and personal faith into crystal-clear focus. Her ability to see so deeply and in such precise detail and to describe what she had seen so accurately is all the more remarkable because Fanny was blind. This handicap was made all the more profound because it did not have to happen.

Fanny Jane Crosby was born in Putnam County, New York, on March 24, 1820. When she was six weeks old she developed a cold that caused an inflammation in her eyes. Fanny was in obvious pain, she cried constantly, and her appetite was poor. Naturally the family turned to those around them to find a way to bring their child some relief. A well-meaning stranger recommended the use of hot poultices applied directly to the eyes,

assuring them he had seen this work. The Crosbys jumped at this chance to cure their child and prepared the treatment. Rather than cure Fanny, the poultices all but destroyed her eyesight. Because of the amateur medical advice, a girl who was born with perfect vision spent the remainder of her life in darkness.

During the early days of the United States, blindness, like almost all other handicaps, was considered a curse. Many Christians felt that those afflicted in such a way were being punished by God. Thus most severely handicapped children were rarely seen. They were hidden away or sent off to sanitariums. They certainly were not educated, nor did they mix with "normal" people. They were also not expected to make any contributions to society. Children with handicaps were seen by most as being without value and as an embarrassment.

The death of Crosby's father, coming less than a year after her birth, put extra pressure on the family. Now her mother and siblings had the burden of making a living in addition to taking care of a child with a major physical handicap. Yet in spite of these new demands placed on the Crosbys, Fanny was not pushed into the background and treated as a burden. To the contrary, Crosby was raised in an environment where she was not pitied or ignored. She never heard the words, "You can't do that because you are blind." In fact, even when Crosby was very young, her grandmother suggested Fanny's condition meant that God had some very important work for her to do. So she was educated, given chores, and encouraged to dream.

It was no doubt because of her family's attitude toward her blindness that Crosby wrote these words when just nine years old.

Oh what a happy soul I am,
Although I cannot see;
I am resolved that in this world
Contented I will be.
How many blessings I enjoy,
That other people don't;
To weep and sigh because I'm blind,
I cannot, and I won't.

Even though Crosby was surrounded by love and treated as an equal member of her family, her disability put limits on her life. Fanny could not attend school because education during this time did not have the tools to deal with her special needs. But this roadblock did not keep the Crosby family from seeking out other ways to present knowledge to the girl. They found local teachers who revamped their teaching style in order to work with Fanny one-on-one. These instructors soon discovered that this blind girl, who lived in a world of darkness, was one of the brightest children they had ever known.

Fanny progressed through standard education much more quickly than her peers. By the age of twelve she could recite a good portion of the Bible, knew volumes of great literature and poetry, could work complex math problems, and had a solid knowledge of history. Much more than other children she also seemed to understand the nature of people. Yet, even though she was mature beyond her years and remained outwardly positive, she longed to be treated less like a novelty and more like a real person. Her nightly prayer became "I want to be able to learn like normal children."

By the time she was fourteen, Crosby's life had taken on a routine. She studied with teachers when they had the time to

work with her, attended church, did the same household chores each day, and, when she could, stole away to compose poetry. She memorized her verses and later shared them with the few people in the Crosby family's circle of friends. Though outwardly happy, Fanny felt stifled. Just like the candle she could sense but not see, she felt there was a larger light out there beckoning her to come bask in its glow.

Crosby did not speak to her teachers of being able to do what normal children did. She shared this desire only with family. Fanny told them she knew she would never be able to see, but she feared that because of this fact she would soon grow to a point where she would no longer be able to learn. She wanted to explore the world, but she sensed she would probably never leave the area where she was being raised. Blindness, it seemed, was keeping her in the dark.

At the urging of teachers, the Crosby family began to look for a way to more fully develop Fanny's talents. Though realizing a rural girl had little chance of winning acceptance, her mother wrote to the New York Institute for the Blind. In her correspondence, she shared her little girl's story. The head of the school studied the letter as well as recommendations from Fanny's teachers. He was impressed by both, but also by the samples of Fanny's writing that had been included with the letters. Probably due more to her poems than her knowledge of history and the Bible, the school found a way to admit Crosby.

Fanny left her home, heading toward what she saw as the light that was drawing her — a light so faint others could not perceive it, but in her mind as bright as the sun itself. She later wrote, "That was the happiest day of my life. The dark intellectual maze in which I had been living seemed to yield to hope with the promise of the light that was about to dawn. I did not

$\mathcal{N}$ear the Cross

Jesus, keep me near the cross,
There a precious fountain,
Free to all — a healing stream,
Flows from Calvary's mountain.

Near the cross, a trembling soul,
Love and mercy found me;
There the Bright and Morning Star
Sheds its beams around me.

Near the cross! O Lamb of God,
Bring its scenes before me;
Help me walk from day to day,
With its shadows over me.

Near the cross I'll watch and wait,
Hoping, trusting ever,
Till I reach the golden strand,
Just beyond the river.

Refrain
In the cross, in the cross,
Be my glory ever;
Till my raptured soul shall find
Rest beyond the river.

crave bodily vision; it was mental enlightenment I sought." As she quickly discovered, the spark she was seeking at the school would grow into a mighty fire; it would enlarge her world and offer opportunities of which she had never dreamed, yet in itself it would not be totally satisfying.

Crosby stayed at the School for the Blind for the next twenty-three years, the first eight as a student. When she had learned all that could be taught by the institute, she was offered a job as a teacher. As dynamic as had been her performance as a student, it was overshadowed by the skills and energy she brought to the position of instructor.

In the midst of her new life, Fanny retained one element of her childhood: the continuing urge to write. Working with instructors, then with editors, she improved her prose to the point where magazines began to buy her work. While she was still a teacher at the institute, two of her books of poetry were published and distributed across the nation. Thus, even as she taught blind children how to cope with the never-changing darkness, Crosby was living a long-held dream of finding a place of acceptance in the sighted world. Though this brought much more recognition than she ever believed she would achieve, the spotlight was not completely satisfying. Fanny soon realized it was not the one she had left home to find. But that light she sought was closer than she could have guessed.

One night Crosby left campus and walked to an evening service at a New York Methodist Church. The message moved her, but it was only when she heard the words of Isaac Watts's hymn "At the Cross" that Crosby saw the real light for the first time. Not only did she get up and find her way to the front of the sanctuary to rededicate her life to the Lord, but she also

vowed to turn her writing skills in a new direction. Now she would write for Jesus.

In 1858, Crosby married another blind teacher, Alexander Van Alstyne. A talented musician, Fanny's husband encouraged her to continue to compose poetry, giving her the freedom to fully develop her talents and skills in the manner she felt best. No longer teaching, the new wife had the time to create lyrics for hymns. Inspired by the likes of master songwriters such as Watts and Wesley, she put a new world, straightforward spring on gospel poetry. Her work was so different and fresh that within two years her religious poetry was embraced by a number of publishers and composers. One of the men calling at her door was W. B. Bradbury, the composer of music for "Jesus Loves Me," "Solid Rock," and "Sweet Hour of Prayer." The Bradbury-Crosby team remained in place for five years, creating scores of new hymns. Then, when Bradbury died in 1868, Fanny continued to write with Philip Phillips, Hubert P. Main, Ira D. Sankey, Philip P. Bliss, and W. F. Sherwin. The giants of the music industry found this woman's vision was clearer than any lyricist they had ever met. With her cowriters Fanny composed "Blessed Assurance," "He Hideth My Soul," "Draw Me Nearer," "I Am Thine, O Lord," "Jesus Is Tenderly Calling," "Praise Him, Praise Him," "Rescue the Perishing," and hundreds of other timeless hymns. To her cowriters Crosby's ability to create lyrics with such great meaning was beyond comprehension, but what overshadowed this talent was her ability to keep doing it day after day, year after year.

William H. Doane was twelve years Crosby's junior. Like Crosby, the Preston, Connecticut, native seemed always positive and upbeat. His joy for life showed in his eyes, and his energy was evident in his every step. Though a musical prodigy,

he became the head of a large woodworking machinery plant, composing music only as a hobby. He probably never would have been published if he had not worked with evangelist Dwight L. Moody during the latter's Ohio crusades. Soon Doane was scoring songs for Moody, and after the evangelist published some of the industrialist's work, Doane was introduced to Fanny Crosby.

For four decades Doane sent Crosby arrangements of his newest compositions. Rarely pressing the woman, he would allow her to study the feel and mood found in each individual piece. He would then patiently wait as his music spoke to the writer. Such was the way Fanny Crosby's only real Easter song was created.

In 1869, Doane gave Crosby an arrangement that, when played, immediately transported the blind woman to the cross where Jesus was crucified. As always happened when she received inspiration, she visualized a new experience. No matter that she could not remember ever seeing, or that she had no concept of colors, shadows, or light, Fanny saw each new experience in great detail. Such was surely the case with the lyrics she created for "Near the Cross."

The imagery in this song came from a blind woman's heart rather than her eyes, but she saw the gospel far more clearly than most. Her words are not the abstract ramblings of one trying to understand something she has never seen; they are the vision of a real cross and the message of the one who was nailed on that cross. Somehow, Crosby literally witnessed it, and then, in simple terms, also painted it so that sighted people might see it as clearly as she did. In each verse the imagery of the shadow of the cross, the beam of heavenly light, and the feeling of warmth created by Christ's love are revealed in

images that only a sighted person could describe. Yet Fanny saw it too.

Like scores of other Crosby hymns, "Near the Cross" immediately found its way into hymnbooks and hearts. It still illuminates Easter as few hymns can. It clearly presents the genius of the writer, one who was, in her day, considered to be the greatest songwriter in America. One biographer wrote, "Johann Strauss reigned in Vienna as the 'Waltz King,' and John Philip Sousa in Washington as the 'March King,' so Fanny Crosby reigned in New York in the later nineteenth and early twentieth century as the 'Hymn Queen.' "

Crosby lived ninety-five years, enjoying every moment of her time on earth. One of the questions she was asked most was, "Do you wish there was an operation that would enable you to see?" She would always laugh at this question, then respond by saying, "No, I have been blessed by my blindness. Because of it, the first face I will see will be my Savior's."

Fanny Crosby spent thirty-eight years chasing the light she thought she could find in education, then in teaching others. Though these experiences gave her a sense of accomplishment, they did not illuminate her world in a way that brought lasting satisfaction. Then, one night in a church service, she discovered that to walk in the light she longed for, she had to be "Near the Cross." Because she made that journey, millions of others have heard her words and followed her example to that same cross.

I Gave My Life for Thee

*T*he two people responsible for an Easter hymn that challenges Christians to give something back as thanks for Christ's gift on the cross came from very different backgrounds. In fact beyond their faith, Frances Ridley Havergal and Philip Bliss really could be connected only by their burning desire to compose spiritual music and by a man named Dwight L. Moody. Though Havergal and Bliss never met, this thin connection was enough to allow their talents to merge on the moving tribute to Christ's sacrifice for sinners, "I Gave My Life for Thee."

Havergal was born in 1836 in Astley in Worcestershire, England. Her father was an Anglican priest who rose to the office of canon during his daughter's childhood. Thus Frances's early years were filled with all the obligations and rebellion usually associated with being a preacher's kid. Carefree, happy, and outgoing, she thought little of faith until 1848. At the age of twelve, Frances was called to her cancer-stricken mother's bed. The dying woman begged her daughter to please become a child of God and live her faith each day of her life.

Frances idolized her mother. She knew that during her short life this woman had given everything she could to her family

and her God. Now she wondered what she could do to live up to her mother's example. Seized by this challenge and fueled by the knowledge of how fragile life could be, the young girl immediately went to work. While others her age were playing with dolls, Frances was organizing local young people in Bible study groups, doing needlework to raise funds for mission work, and writing religious poetry. Even when she went on vacations, she looked for ways to grow in her faith. In her late teens Havergal accompanied her father to Germany. On the trip she bought several religious books. Upon her return to England, she read them and then set them aside, but several years later she rediscovered one of these vacation souvenirs.

Havergal was constantly on the go, always involved in projects that furthered God's work in her area. Gifted with an outstanding voice, she was in great demand as a vocalist, often being called to London to perform in large churches there. While still in her twenties, she was very well known in England's religious community for her charity work and her vocal talents. Many of the great scholars and preachers of the day, including American evangelist Dwight L. Moody, corresponded with the young woman. However it was not while in a great cathedral or while visiting with a renowned church leader that Havergal's greatest inspiration hit her. On January 10, 1858, Havergal came back to the family home exhausted after spending another day involved in mission fundraising work. To remove the chill from her body, she sat in a chair by the roaring fire. As she rocked she happened to note a book she had purchased during her trip to Germany. Picking it up, she aimlessly flipped through the pages until a drawing of Jesus dying on the cross caught her attention. Under the illustration was the question, "What have you done for me?"

Retrieving a pencil and a scrap of paper, Havergal jotted down her thoughts on the question. She read her words several times, made some additional notes, then set the paper aside. Picking up her Bible, she leafed through various New Testament Scriptures, carefully studying each of them before returning to her poem. Reading her new work again, she shook her head. "This is poor," she sighed to her sister before getting up and tossing the paper into the fire.

When Frances left the room, Maria noted that somehow the composition had been blown out of the blazing fireplace and was now resting unscathed on the floor. Retrieving it, she set it aside, then later in the day gave it back to her sister. Frances looked over her poem again and passed it on to her father. Impressed, the elder Havergal wrote a simple tune to go with "I Gave My Life for Thee" and had it printed in leaflet form. This version made its way to America a decade later.

In 1868, Philip Paul Bliss was thirty years old. His life was already the stuff of a best-selling fiction novel. Born to a poor family on a Pennsylvania farm, he left home at the age of eleven because the family could not feed him. Starting with just two pennies in his pocket, Bliss found jobs on farms, scrambling to eke out a living while traveling the dusty roads of the eastern United States. For six years he constantly evaded robbers, disease, and starvation. He was a hungry teen on a cold night in 1850 when he wandered into a Baptist revival meeting. After hearing the message, he gave his life to God. Even though he would later speak of the joy flooding his heart at that moment, his world was still far from perfect. After all, he was still homeless and hungry. So the next day he was out again looking for work.

In between his jobs, Bliss snuck into schools. At night, using borrowed books, he furthered his education by candlelight.

I Gave My Life for Thee

I gave my life for thee
My precious blood I shed
That thou might'st ransomed be
And raised up from the dead
I gave, I gave my life for thee:
What has thou giv'n for me?

My Father's house of light
My glory circled throne
I left for earthly night
For wand'rings sad and lone
I left, I left it all for thee:
Has thou left aught for me?

And I have brought to thee
Down from my home above
Salvation full and free
My pardon and my love
I bring, I bring rich gifts to thee:
What hast thou brought to me?

Within a few years he had somehow learned enough about reading, writing, and arithmetic to talk his way into a teaching position in Almond, New York. There he found more than just a steady paycheck; he also discovered the love of his life and married the school board president's daughter.

At about this same time Bliss attended a singing convention in Rome, Pennsylvania. This seemingly unimportant event dramatically altered the young man's life. After meeting W. B. Bradbury, composer of such songs as "Savior Like a Shepherd Lead Us" and "Sweet Hour of Prayer," and George Root, who had given the world "Jesus Loves the Little Children," Bliss became consumed with a desire to serve God through music. He began to compose his own hymns, staying in touch with Bradbury and Root. Accepting an invitation to move to Chicago to work for Root set this quest for ministry in motion, but another chance meeting with another gospel giant fully cemented Bliss's place in the Christian world.

In 1869, Bliss and his wife were strolling past the Windy City's Wood's Museum Theatre. World-famous evangelist Dwight L. Moody was on the steps of the theater inviting those walking by to come in and listen to his message. Not only did Bliss accept the invitation, but his robust voice caught the evangelist's attention. A few weeks later Bliss was leading singing for Moody's services.

With the Moody connection, Bliss's original music premiered at huge revival meetings, and scores of his songs were published through the evangelist's organization. He had not so much found his calling as it had found him. In 1871, the music Bliss wrote for Horatio B. Spafford's "It Is Well with My Soul" made him famous all over the world. Suddenly Bliss was in demand, often leaving his wife and children for weeks at a

time to sing and teach music across America. By 1876, Moody wanted to take Bliss to England. It was an exciting time for the once lonely farm boy.

It was probably during his days with Moody that Bliss was given a copy of Havergal's simple hymn. The evangelist wanted fresh music to go with the inspired lyrics of "I Gave My Life for Thee." Bliss had little trouble creating the new music, and Moody immediately began to use this version in his crusades.

In December of that year the family spent Christmas with Bliss's mother in Rome, Pennsylvania. Soon after this holiday celebration, Bliss and his wife left their children with a family member as they returned to Chicago in time for a New Year's Eve crusade at the Moody Tabernacle. In a blinding snowstorm their train approached Ashtaula, Ohio. Bliss was working on scoring a new song in an almost empty dining car when he heard a groan and felt a sudden sideways movement. A few seconds later eleven train cars plunged off a bridge and into a seventy-foot ravine. Because of their blazing stoves, each of these wooden cars burst into flames.

According to other survivors, Bliss was tossed clear of the wreckage, miraculously finding himself safe in the snow. But when he noticed the car where his wife had been riding was ablaze, he rushed into the fiery carnage to save her. He was never seen again. When rescue teams combed the wreckage, they found neither Bliss nor his wife. Both had been completely consumed by the flames. Several days after Bliss died, a trunk arrived in Chicago. It had been on one of the cars that did not go down when the bridge collapsed. Inside that piece of baggage was a song Bliss had recently composed. The hymn "I Will Sing of My Redeemer" reflected the passion that drove Bliss's life. It was a fitting tribute.

Three years after Bliss tragically died, Frances Ridley Havergal was getting ready to join Dwight L. Moody for his English crusade. She was to be the featured singer. However as she prepared to leave, the forty-two-year-old woman grew feverish. A doctor diagnosed peritonitis, and a cable was sent to Moody informing him that Havergal's condition was hopeless. Writhing in pain, Frances called out to her family and asked to take communion. It seemed a strange request for a Protestant. Caught by surprise, her brothers and sister seemed hesitant until Frances explained there was no better time to remember the Savior who had died for her than when she too was dying. After partaking of the bread and wine, Frances asked those gathered to sing one of her songs. They chose "Take My Life and Let It Be." She died as the last words rang out.

Neither the lyricist nor the music composer lived long enough to fully comprehend the power of the song they had penned together, nor did they realize their hymn would soon annually close thousands of Easter services all around the globe. But as the popularity of the song spread, those who knew the writers realized these two did more than create one of the most haunting Easter hymns; they lived the song's message each day of their lives. In fact, Frances Havergal and Philip Bliss are still challenging others to give their lives to the Lord through "I Gave My Life for Thee."

11

Hallelujah! Christ Is Risen

*I*t is a sad fact of history that few born with well-known names manage to live up to the expectations of that name. Such was not the case with Christopher Wordsworth. The nephew of noted poet William Wordsworth, Christopher rose through the ranks of English scholars to become one of the most respected theologians and writers of his era. Today he is best known not for his commentaries on the Bible and church doctrines but rather for composing the lyrics to one of the world's best Easter anthems.

Born in 1807, as a child Christopher was not only scholarly but also a great athlete. He was known as much for his play on the cricket field as for his marks in the classroom. Still, in the early 1800s it was brains and not brawn that offered the surest path to success. So after a stint at Cambridge, Wordsworth left behind the grassy fields of sport to become a teacher. Soon he also assumed the mantle of Anglican priest and by 1844 had been appointed canon of Westminster Abbey. Six years later, he left the famed Abbey to serve as the pastor of a church in rural England, where within two decades he earned the title

of bishop. In that role he exhibited great influence over church doctrine and worship practices.

During his life Wordsworth was best known for his intellectual religious treatises, but from time to time he also gave himself over to the Wordsworth family tradition of poetry. As he felt most modern hymns were biblically inaccurate and not reverent enough for worship services, he often opted to create poems based on passages of Scripture that supported long-held church practices. Though conservative, Wordsworth did accept the premise first pushed by Isaac Watts that songs could be produced without relying solely on inspiration found in the book of Psalms. Still, the bishop did not adhere to the position that hymns should ever include personal testimonies such as Watts had employed while writing "When I Survey the Wondrous Cross." Wordsworth viewed these types of compositions as little more than folk ditties with no real meaning in congregational worship. He believed this so strongly that he felt all personal testimony songs, including the popular "Amazing Grace," should be removed from all Anglican hymnals.

Sensing a need for an Easter hymn expressing what he saw as the proper biblical view of the day, Wordsworth was drawn to Matthew 28:6. This verse, combined with a lifetime of experience in the church, was all he needed for inspiration: "He is not here: for he is risen, as he said. Come, see the place where the Lord lay."

Adhering strictly to Wordsworth's beliefs, "Hallelujah! Christ Is Risen" celebrated a risen Savior in a way that was true to the biblical view but was still presented in a manner inclusive of the entire church body. Most important to Wordsworth, it was not the personal testimony of just a single believer. Matched with a very formal tune, the hymn found its way into print in

the middle part of the nineteenth century. While used by some churches in Britain, it was hardly as popular as the personal hymns the bishop had meant it to replace.

James McGranahan was born about the same time that Wordsworth became a bishop. Gifted with a three-octave range, he began to study opera in the 1860s. For more than a decade the young man sought out the best teachers to enhance his chances of becoming one of the nation's best-known classical stars. But a letter and a train wreck derailed his dreams and refocused his energies on a higher calling.

In 1877, between stage auditions, McGranahan was employed as a music teacher at George Root's National Normal Institute in Lebanon, Ohio. Just before Christmas, McGranahan received a letter from noted Christian songwriter and evangelist Philip Bliss. Bliss, who had known McGranahan for more than a decade, wrote to ask James to reconsider his career path. Bliss felt McGranahan would be happier and more fulfilled if he used his voice for evangelism.

McGranahan was touched by the admiration Bliss had for his talents, but he had no intention of turning his back on opera. He felt that only through classical music could his full potential be realized. He remained unbending in this conviction until one week later. Via a telegram, McGranahan learned that Bliss and his wife had been involved in a violent train crash while on their way to sing with evangelist Dwight L. Moody at a New Year's Eve rally in Chicago.

McGranahan rushed to the scene in hopes of helping to find survivors. The death and destruction he witnessed in that snowy Ohio valley were sobering. He had never even imagined such a devastating tragedy. As he and other volunteers sorted through the carnage, he wondered who would pick up

the mantle left by Bliss's passing. Considering this huge void in the world of Christian music, he looked at his own life. Bliss had been joyful and happy, always fulfilled and never struggling to be accepted. Meanwhile, McGranahan encountered constant rejection as time and time again he was told his talents did not measure up to operatic standards. With his feet trampling through deep snow and his cold hands sifting through wreckage, he reordered his life. The next day, even as he mourned the loss of his friend, McGranahan found himself strangely happy, so much so he picked up pen and paper and composed the beginning of "There Shall Be Showers of Blessing." This beloved hymn was the first step in McGranahan's three-decade-long career in Christian music.

During his worldwide evangelistic travels, McGranahan was introduced to Wordsworth's hymn "Hallelujah! Christ Is Risen." The singer felt the words were inspired, but he believed the original tune lacked real passion. It seemed far too stiff to reach the hearts of those who sang the powerful words. Developing a new melody, then arranging it for congregational singing, McGranahan introduced his version of the English bishop's Easter hymn. In large part because of McGranahan's powerful vocal performances, this new version of "Hallelujah! Christ Is Risen" quickly gained popularity as a congregational standard. Long before McGranahan's death in 1907, his version of the Wordsworth hymn was accepted by most churches in America and around the world.

Christopher Wordsworth once wrote, "It is the first duty of a hymn to teach sound doctrine and thence to save souls." In its original form his "Hallelujah! Christ Is Risen" accomplished the first part of this goal. But because Wordsworth was so much at war with the musical revolution of his day, he failed to deliver a

ℋallelujah! Christ Is Risen

Hallelujah! Hallelujah!
Heart and voice to heaven raise,
Sing to God a hymn of gladness,
Sing to God a hymn of praise;
He who on the cross a ransom
For the world's salvation bled,
Jesus Christ the King of glory
Now is risen from the dead.

Christ is risen, Christ the firstfruits
Of the holy harvest field,
Which will all its full abundance,
At his glorious advent, yield;
Then the golden ears of harvest
Will before his presence wave,
Rising in his sunshine joyous,
From the furrow of the grave.

Hallelujah! Hallelujah!
Glory be to God above!
Hallelujah, to the Savior,
Fount of life and source of love;
Hallelujah, to the Spirit
Let our high ascriptions be;
Hallelujah, now and ever,
To the blessèd Trinity.

hymn that appealed to the masses. A half a world away, James McGranahan remade the bishop's work into a song that still reaches millions each Easter. While Wordsworth might not have agreed with this more personal tune, it allowed "Hallelujah! Christ Is Risen" to fully realize the bishop's goal as a composer, a theologian, and a preacher.

The Tradition of Sunrise Services

In the end of the sabbath, as it began to dawn toward the first day of the week, came Mary Magdalene and the other Mary to see the sepulchre. And, behold, there was a great earthquake: for the angel of the Lord descended from heaven, and came and rolled back the stone from the door, and sat upon it. His countenance was like lightning, and his raiment white as snow: And for fear of him the keepers did shake, and became as dead men.

And the angel answered and said unto the women, Fear not ye: for I know that ye seek Jesus, which was crucified. He is not here: for he is risen, as he said. Come, see the place where the Lord lay. And go quickly, and tell his disciples that he is risen from the dead; and, behold, he goeth before you into Galilee; there shall ye see him: lo, I have told you.

And they departed quickly from the sepulchre with fear and great joy; and did run to bring his disciples word. And as they went to tell his disciples, behold, Jesus met them, saying, All hail. And they came and held him by the feet, and worshipped him.

— Matthew 28:1 – 9

*I*magine the emotions of the two Marys that morning. As the dawn broke and sunlight began to flood their world, what must they have been thinking? They had come to pay homage to a close friend who had died; they had witnessed him being executed, and now they find that their friend is alive! Their initial reaction was probably disbelief, but when they saw him and heard his voice, they did what was natural; they fell to their knees in prayer and thanksgiving.

Surely that moment, just outside the tomb, was the first Christian sunrise service. It also has to have been one of the most moving experiences of all time, yet the Bible does not mention anyone else ever gathering at dawn to mark Christ's victory over the grave. Neither Paul, John, Thomas, Andrew, nor one of the Marys is ever again linked to a sunrise service. Hence, there is no Bible directive for gathering in the early hours of Easter morning.

Doubtless those who witnessed that first Easter morning probably returned to the tomb many times. After all, it is the nature of human beings to come back to places where they experienced something uplifting. So even without historians recording it, logic dictates that the two Marys, as well as other followers of Jesus, would have been drawn to the tomb at sunrise on the anniversary of the resurrection. This spot where they first saw a risen Christ would surely be to them the most important place on earth.

In a period when a host of edicts were presented to ensure uniform worship, there is no record of dictates concerning sunrise services on Easter. In ancient pagan customs, worshipers often gathered before the dawn each spring to welcome back the sun god. As missionaries converted tribes to Christianity, they tried to get new believers to discard any old customs tied

too closely to pagan worship. Hence, the Easter sunrise services might well have been ignored during the early days of missionary work to ensure they not be confused with old pagan rituals. Yet as time passed and Christianity became well established, some churches began to gather early on Easter morning to retrace the steps of the two Marys.

Just as it is now, scriptural symbolism, such as was found in reenacting the moment when Christ's resurrection was first witnessed, was a great and powerful teaching tool. Simply meeting in the moments before dawn on Easter Sunday allowed Jesus' conquering the grave to become more real to believers. Most of the churches that adopted these services usually held them outside, some even in graveyards. In this environment many came to believe in a risen Christ.

Though not officially required by church leaders, sunrise services in varying forms continued through the Dark and Middle Ages until the Reformation. While the practice of a sunrise Mass continued in many Catholic churches as well as in Protestant churches in Central and Eastern Europe, the more conservative denominations springing up in Great Britain and America did not engage in dawn services on Easter. In fact they ignored the holiday altogether.

In the United States sunrise services and Easter did not become established until the middle of the nineteenth century. The timing could not have been better. With so many Americans dying in the Civil War, many men and women felt drawn to these morning services as a way to have their faith renewed. To the depressed family members, the symbolism of the dark of night being conquered by the sun's light was a great comfort.

Newspapers contain many stories of church sunrise services throughout the rest of the 1800s, but in the early 1900s the

concept really took off. Now not only did churches schedule sunrise services to mark the moment of the resurrection, but so did many communities. By the 1920s thousands were turning out in places like Colorado Springs to relive what the two Marys witnessed firsthand on the morning Christ arose. Still, except for a few large productions, some complete with actors playing all the principal parts, most sunrise services remained solemn, almost informal, services consisting of Scripture, Easter carols, short messages, and prayers. Some congregations also lit candles at dawn to signify the light that Christ brought to the world.

Today at Easter many churches around the world meet outdoors in the minutes before dawn. There are even services in the Holy Land at the spot where they believe the two Marys first saw a risen Savior. All these services serve as an echo of the most important moment in church history—when death was conquered and the world was greeted with a Sonrise at sunrise.

Beneath the
Cross of Jesus

*E*lizabeth Clephane was born on June 18, 1830, the third daughter of a Scottish lawman. She was never a strong child, prone to long bouts of sickness and therefore often homebound. In spite of her inability to move through life as freely as she would like, Elizabeth had a strong, sweet spirit that deeply touched the community of Melrose. So, in the midst of their hard lives, the people of the village looked upon Elizabeth as an inspiration. She showed that even in the worst of times, joy and wonder can be found in each new day and that every breath is a blessing for which to give thanks.

Taking Clephane's bleak life into account, it is amazing that Elizabeth was able to maintain her positive attitude. Not only was she constantly fighting illness, but her father died when she was just a girl. After his death, times were tough for the family. Even finding enough to eat was often an insurmountable task, and affording medical care for Clephane was simply beyond the family's means. But the fragile girl never complained. In bad times and good, she remained a shining beacon for her siblings as well as an inspiration to those who observed her from afar.

When bouts of illness confined her to the family's tiny home, Clephane turned her attention to reading. Like many from her country, she enthusiastically consumed the works of local hero Sir Walter Scott, but, unlike few outside the clergy, she also spent hours each day reading the Bible. It is hardly surprising that by the time she was in her mid-twenties, her knowledge of English literature was exceeded only by her understanding of the Good Book. The latter, much more than the former, influenced everything she did. Many claimed they could actually feel Christ's love in her gentle touch.

Clephane's easy smile lit up every room she entered. In fact, most in Melrose called her not by her given name, but by her nickname, "Sunbeam." And, on those days when she was healthy enough to leave her home, it was as Sunbeam that the slight woman made her rounds sharing food and clothing with the poor as well as tending the sick and elderly. Doing these menial chores brought her more happiness than anything in her sparse life.

While it is impossible to say if Clephane felt a foreshadowing of her own early passing, there can be no doubt that she well understood the fragile nature of life. She had ministered to the gravely ill of all ages. She had watched her father die in the prime of his life. She had seen children taken just after birth and had held the hands of the elderly as they drew their final breaths. Just as she knew hunger, despair, and poverty, she knew death. Thus, as she reached out to those whose every moment was filled with pain and suffering, she felt driven to share the story of faith that made her life so meaningful and her own pain so meaningless. In that way she transcended being "Sunbeam" and became a beam of light from God's own Son.

By 1868, Clephane's body was further weakened by numerous bouts with the flu, her vision was starting to fail, and she

looked much older than her thirty-eight years. Nevertheless, though her back was bent and her frame was rail thin, her smile was as quick as ever, and there was still a sparkle in her eyes. Yet, though still a young woman, Clephane had to have known she was near death's door. It was probably for that reason she seemed so intent on making each new day count for something special. Even when she was confined to her bed, she seemed to be constantly looking for ways to leave behind the essence of her faith to future generations. Like her hero Scott, she would touch others with timeless verse.

One afternoon, as she laid aside her well-worn Bible and picked up a pencil, Clephane considered several essential elements of her faith. The first was that Christ was her rock and had saved and delivered her from the travails of an existence filled with sin and temptation. After all, she had seen many unhappy souls who had given in to temptation only to be tortured by it. Through faith she had escaped that fate. Next she considered the suffering Christ had endured in order to give her the blessings of a forgiven life. This led her to consider the unworthiness of all people, including herself. That Jesus had died for her, when he could have chosen not to, humbled her beyond measure. She felt awed by God's grace.

As Clephane thought of Christ's suffering on the cross, she turned from the horrid scene to the results of that painful death. Because of the cross, she had been given the keys to God's kingdom. She had received the joy and comfort of having him with her during bad times and good and had come to appreciate the promise of eternal life. Hence, the cross was in fact not a dark moment in time, but one of the brightest in human history. It was the conduit to experiencing the eternal love of God.

Opening her Bible, Clephane read Matthew 27:36–37: "And sitting down they watched him there; and set up over his head his accusation written, THIS IS JESUS THE KING OF THE JEWS." These were not new verses to her. She had read them hundreds of times. But today this Scripture brought her the greatest inspiration she had ever known in her short life. Elizabeth was transported to the cross and had a vision for a poem. In only a few years, the five verses she wrote would become one of the most important songs the church would use throughout Lent and on Easter. Yet on this day, the words Clephane penned were just a vehicle the woman employed to spell out what Christ meant to her. This poem was for her eyes only; it was for her heart, and it was to anchor her faith.

When she finished writing "Beneath the Cross of Jesus," Clephane did nothing with it. Satisfied that her writing had brought her closer to her Lord, she filed her latest work away with seven other Christian poems. These eight poems were discovered after Clephane died, and for a short while they were shared with just family and friends. Initially no one thought of taking them to the world. Then, in 1872, a family member submitted them to the Scottish Presbyterian periodical *Family Treasury*. The editor published Clephane's poems one at a time under the title *Breathing on the Borders*. The first printed was "Beneath the Cross of Jesus," and no writer credit was given. As Clephane did not want to bask in the spotlight, she would have probably approved of not being spotlighted as the poem's writer. This humble woman would have wanted readers to dwell not on her often sad and short life but rather on the life, death, and resurrection of her Savior.

It is not known whether composer Frederick Charles Maker first saw Clephane's poem in the *Family Treasury* or if he spotted

Beneath the Cross
of Jesus

Beneath the cross of Jesus I fain would take my stand,
The shadow of a mighty rock within a weary land;
A home within the wilderness, a rest upon the way,
From the burning of the noontide heat, and the burden of the day.

O safe and happy shelter, O refuge tried and sweet,
O trysting place where heaven's love and heaven's justice meet!
As to the holy patriarch that wondrous dream was given,
So seems my Savior's cross to me, a ladder up to heaven.

There lies beneath its shadow but on the further side
The darkness of an awful grave that gapes both deep and wide
And there between us stands the cross two arms outstretched to save
A watchman set to guard the way from that eternal grave.

Upon that cross of Jesus mine eye at times can see
The very dying form of one who suffered there for me;
And from my stricken heart with tears two wonders I confess;
The wonders of redeeming love and my unworthiness.

I take, O cross, thy shadow for my abiding place;
I ask no other sunshine than the sunshine of his face;
Content to let the world go by to know no gain or loss,
My sinful self my only shame, my glory all the cross.

it when it was later reprinted in a British newspaper. Whichever is the case, when the forty-year-old composer read the words to "Beneath the Cross of Jesus," he was deeply moved. Maker, an organist, a professor of music at Clifton College, and the conductor of the Bristol Free Church Choir, felt this dynamic testimony could reach a much larger audience if it could be sung. Therefore, Maker created a musical score for the poem and entitled his new melody "St. Christopher." As it was written during an era when modern music was being accepted into English worship, this coupling of verse and melody quickly made "Beneath the Cross of Jesus" one of the most popular hymns in British church history. When contrasted against Elizabeth Clephane's weak body and humble existence, the song's power and majesty takes on even deeper meaning.

When first anonymously published in *Family Treasury*, Elizabeth Clephane's poems created so much reader feedback that Reverend W. Arnot, the periodical's editor, felt moved to share something of the writer's personality and character. He wrote, "These lines express the experiences, the hopes, and the longings of a young Christian lately released. Written on the very edge of life, with the better land fully in view of faith, they seem to us footsteps printed on the sands of time, where these sands touch the ocean of Eternity. These footprints of one whom the Good Shepherd led through the wilderness into rest, may, with God's blessing, contribute to comfort and direct succeeding pilgrims." And so they have!

Almost a century and a half later, Elizabeth Clephane's words have done more than even Arnot could have imagined. They have led people not just to view the cross but also to understand its meaning. This frail woman's example continues to touch lost souls with the glory of the cross, and Sunbeam became a ray of spiritual light for the world.

Crown Him with
Many Crowns

*M*ost Easter hymns were inspired by verses found in the four gospels. Yet as strange as it may seem, one of the season's most powerful songs drew its initial inspiration from the final book in the Bible: "His eyes were as a flame of fire, and on his head were many crowns; and he had a name written, that no man knew, but he himself" (Revelation 19:12).

When John wrote Revelation, he was living as an exile on the island of Patmos. While confined to this obscure piece of earth, John was visited by visions from heaven. What he saw and heard was wilder than any fictional story ever written. What he witnessed was probably beyond the imagination of any person living at that time. Given a glimpse into the future, John initially collapsed in fear, but ultimately he preserved his amazing vision in writing.

On Patmos John witnessed a battle between the forces of the greatest evil and the greatest good in the universe. A New Jerusalem, perfect in every way, resulted from this cosmic war, and the Lord God Almighty and the Lamb were the temple of this beautiful city. As John saw every race and tribe of people

worshiping Jesus as one, he knew how the prophecy of Christ would be ultimately realized. At a time when royal families ruled so many places on earth, John realized that Jesus was the King of Kings.

It took three different writers, each working from their own unique viewpoints, one an Anglican priest, another a former member of the Church of England who became a Catholic, and the last a close friend of the British crown, to take what John wrote and create "Crown Him with Many Crowns." Working separately and at different times spanning almost a quarter of a century, this trio produced an Easter anthem that seamlessly reviews every facet of Christ's life and all the crowns this Savior wears.

The first man in the trio inspired by Revelation 19:12 was Matthew Bridges. Born in 1800 in Sidmouth, England, Bridges was educated in Anglican schools and was a devout member of the Church of England for forty-eight years. Yet when the poet and writer began to study the words of John Henry Newman, he shocked both friends and family by joining the Roman Catholic Church. Three years after converting to Catholicism, Bridges found himself studying John's words in Revelation.

A deeply religious man, Bridges was also an avid student of history and politics. As such he found confrontation not only interesting but also an important element of shaping history. In books of war and rebellion, Bridges saw not just political gains and losses, but man's often tempestuous relationship with God. Therefore, Revelation, a book that frightens many Bible students because it deals with unimaginable horrors and the greatest war of all time, fascinated and inspired Bridges.

Jesus as Lord was central in Bridges' faith. Therefore, spurred on by what he read in Revelation, he wrote "Crown Him with Many Crowns" based on the complex but all-inclusive image of

of the God he found in John's vision. He fleshed out his verses using additional inspiration from Revelation 5:11 – 12, Romans 6:9 – 10, John 20:20, Isaiah 6:2, and Isaiah 9:6. The result was a poem spotlighting Bridges' deep faith and John's incredible vision, one of the most powerful views of Christ ever written. So it is not surprising that when it was published, one prominent composer was so impressed with "Crown Him with Many Crowns" that he felt called to set it to music.

George Job Elvey was born in the famous town of Canterbury, England, on March 27, 1816. He was a natural musician who by the time he enrolled in grammar school was taking singing lessons at the Canterbury Cathedral. As a teen, Elvey received even more formal instruction at the Royal Academy of Music, and at the tender age of nineteen, his musical knowledge and personal maturity were so great that he was appointed as the master of the boys at St. George's Chapel, Windsor, England. In addition, he was asked to fill the post of church organist. Elvey remained at both of these positions until he retired some five decades later.

At St. George's, Elvey often mingled with royalty. At one time or another all the British monarchy heard him perform. Because of the quality of his performances, the young man from Canterbury found himself in the inner circle of English society. So modest was Elvey that until he received a personal summons from the queen he had no idea his original church compositions were making any real impact beyond St. George's. Yet this royal audience positioned him to join a very elite group of Englishmen.

In 1871, Queen Victoria asked Elvey to write the music for an upcoming royal wedding. The composer temporarily cut back his workload at St. George's to labor over a score fit for

Crown Him with Many Crowns

Crown him with many crowns,
    the Lamb upon his throne.
Hark! How the heavenly anthem
    drowns all music but its own.
Awake, my soul, and sing
    of him who died for thee,
And hail him as thy matchless King
    through all eternity.

Crown him the virgin's Son,
    the God incarnate born,
Whose arm those crimson trophies
    won which now his brow adorn;
Fruit of the mystic rose,
    as of that rose the stem;
The root whence mercy ever flows,
    the Babe of Bethlehem.

Crown him the Son of God,
    before the worlds began,
And ye who tread where he hath
    trod, crown him the Son of Man;
Who every grief hath known
    that wrings the human breast,
And takes and bears them for his
    own, that all in him may rest.

Crown him the Lord of life,
    who triumphed over the grave,
And rose victorious in the strife
    for those he came to save.
His glories now we sing,
    who died, and rose on high,
Who died eternal life to bring,
    and lives that death may die.

Crown him the Lord of peace,
    whose power a scepter sways
From pole to pole, that wars may
    cease, and all be prayer and
    praise.
His reign shall know no end,
    and round his piercèd feet
Fair flowers of paradise extend
    their fragrance ever sweet.

Crown him the Lord of love,
    behold his hands and side,
Those wounds, yet visible above,
    in beauty glorified.
No angel in the sky
    can fully bear that sight,

But downward bends his burning eye
at mysteries so bright.

Crown him the Lord of heaven,
enthroned in worlds above,
Crown him the King to whom is given
the wondrous name of Love.
Crown him with many crowns, as
thrones before him fall;
Crown him, ye kings, with many
crowns, for he is King of all.

Crown him the Lord of lords, who over
all doth reign,
Who once on earth, the incarnate
Word, for ransomed sinners slain,
Now lives in realms of light, where
saints with angels sing
Their songs before him day and night,
their God, Redeemer, King.

Crown him the Lord of years, the
Potentate of time,
Creator of the rolling spheres, ineffably
sublime.
All hail, Redeemer, hail! For thou has
died for me;
Thy praise and glory shall not fail
throughout eternity.

(verses 1, 3, 5, & 6 are most
commonly sung today)

a princess. Some weeks later, with great trepidation, he presented his *Festival March* to the crown for review. He wondered if the royals would find his humble music up to the standards needed for this blessed event. He had no cause for fear. The queen and princess were ecstatic.

Those who attended Princess Louise's wedding were deeply impressed with Elvey's *Festival March*. A short time later, the queen knighted Elvey for his thirty-five years of service at St. George's Chapel. Yet *Festival March* would not be Elvey's best loved or most remembered contribution to the world of music.

When Elvey read the newly published "Crown Him with Many Crowns," he felt the poem needed to be set to soaring music. Studying the words very carefully, the composer created a score that could feature the choir at St. George's, along with his organ. He named the new music "Diademata," Greek for "crown," and published it not long after "Crown Him with Many Crowns" had been released as a poem. Elvey's writing the music to go with the words, rather than just matching an existing score to the verses, was a unique approach in England at the time. During this era, most lyrics were simply matched to already published scores. That Bridges' work moved Elvey to compose new music reflects the power of this poem. With its dynamic text and uplifting music, "Crown Him with Many Crowns" seemed complete, and for more than twenty years it remained unchanged. Then, just when Christians on both sides of the Atlantic had memorized the words, some ministers began to cut the hymn from their services.

Because the book of Revelation is so controversial, not all of Bridges' verses sat well with many nineteenth-century biblical scholars. A group of Anglican priests found some of the song's representations of Christ as King not in accordance with their

own views. They wanted to sing about a Savior who was less omnipotent and more loving. Sensing the song was too popular to outright ban, these men of the cloth sought out a priest who was also an accomplished composer. They requested that he create more appropriate words for "Crown Him with Many Crowns."

Godfrey Thring was born in Alford, England, in 1823. He accepted the call of the ministry while still a teen. For the next half century, he preached and wrote hymns such as "Lord of Power, Lord of Might" and "Savior Blessed Savior." Many of his original songs were used by scores of churches in both Britain and the United States. After accepting the task of creating a new version of "Crown Him with Many Crowns," he prayed. Then, before he began to write, he read Bridges' original words and studied the passages in the Bible that dealt with Christ as a king.

It has been written of Thring that he was a man of "clear vision, a firm faith, a positive reality, and an exalting hopefulness." Certainly his version of "Crown Him" exhibited all of those qualities. When it was first published in 1874, he and the clergy who had pressed him to rework the song felt sure that this six-verse version would be forever matched to Elvey's music. Yet, that was not to be the case.

The major hymn publishers didn't jump on the new work or dismiss the old one; instead they carefully studied both versions of "Crown Him with Many Crowns." Most felt that each work had great character and substance. So, rather than choose between them, those editing the songbooks of the day combined the two. They deleted the second and fourth verses of the original, dropping Bridges' inspiration in place of Thring's, then kept the remainder of the original song intact.

In many ways "Crown Him" is unique among all Easter hymns. It is the work of three men who did not know each other and who traveled in different circles. Each brought his own theological views to this special musical offering. Perhaps, as Christ comes to each person in a unique and individual way, this hymn offers a picture of what can happen when the inspiration and faith of one believer is integrated with others. "Crown Him with Many Crowns" is known today because of the combined efforts of three men who discovered that all Christians, no matter how different they are, have one essential element in common: faith in Jesus Christ. And this one element is the most important of all.

15

*C*hrist Arose
(Lo, in the Grave He Lay)

*R*obert Lowry was a man who would rather preach than compose. And why not? Lowry could hold an audience spellbound for hours with his riveting sermons. Today, more than a century after his death, Lowry's dynamic presence in the pulpit has been largely forgotten, while many of his songs remain as fresh as if they had been penned today. One of these favorites, "Christ Arose," dramatically conveys all the complex and varied emotions of those who witnessed the events of the first Easter. In surprisingly simple fashion, this song captures the Passion Week's agony and ecstasy, pain and joy, and depression and exhilaration in a manner that paints a vivid portrait of all that Easter was and is. It is inspired beyond understanding, and yet the hymn brings the holiday to a level even a child can understand.

Robert Lowry was born in Philadelphia on March 12, 1826. The time in which he was raised was one of extremes. The country was expanding at a frenzied rate, the industrial age was about to explode and change the very nature of life for most Americans, and vast waves of immigrants were beginning

their exodus to this new world. Yet amid all of this promise was a dark cloud. Slavery was pulling at the fabric of the United States. It was threatening to end the era of progress by plunging the nation into a catastrophic struggle seething with division and hate. Perhaps because of all this change and emotionally charged conflict, churches began to see great growth as the revival movement started to take off.

Fewer than twenty years before the Civil War, Robert Lowry joined the First Baptist Church of Philadelphia. A scant six years later he felt the call to preach and entered the University of Lewisburg (now Bucknell) to prepare himself for the pulpit. He finished his degree in 1854, and at twenty-eight, Lowry embarked on his new career. Over the course of the next two decades he led congregations in Westchester, Pennsylvania; New York City; Brooklyn; Lewisburg, Pennsylvania; and finally Plainfield, New Jersey.

Though Lowry was an excellent administrator and wonderful pastor, it was his preaching that caused the incredible growth in each of his congregations. Combining his understanding of human nature with a high sense of humor, his messages used words to paint vivid portraits. Crowds were enthralled with the way he brought the gospel to life and the fashion in which he gave understandable personalities to biblical figures. He was a storyteller with great wisdom as well as an entertainer deeply committed to sharing the gospel.

In 1868, one of America's foremost hymnodists, William Bradbury, who composed the music for such great hymns as "He Leadeth Me," "On Christ the Solid Rock I Stand," and "Jesus Loves Me," suddenly died. Bradbury had headed a large music publishing firm that supplied hymnals for thousands of churches. He was a giant in his field. The company, Messrs.

*C*hrist Arose
(Lo, in the Grave He Lay)

Lo, in the grave he lay, Jesus
my Savior,
Waiting the coming day, Jesus
my Lord!

Vainly they watch his bed, Jesus
my Savior;
Vainly they seal the dead, Jesus
my Lord!

Death cannot keep its prey, Jesus
my Savior;
He tore the bars away, Jesus
my Lord!

Refrain
Up from the grave he arose,
With a mighty triumph o'er
his foes,
He arose a victor from the dark
domain,
And he lives forever, with his
saints to reign.
He arose! He arose!
Hallelujah! Christ arose!

Biglow & Main, needed a new leader, and they turned to Robert Lowry. Though he had no formal music training, Lowry accepted the post. This decision would forever alter his life.

Lowry knew little about musical editing. Thus, at an age when most men are looking to retire, he began to study a new field. Nothing would stand in the way of this education, and within months he possessed one of the finest music libraries in the country. He studied for hours each day trying to unlock the secret of how great music was created. At first Lowry tried to blend music and mathematics. To his logical mind it seemed that if middle C had 256 distinct vibrations and all the other notes also had unique but predictable vibration patterns, then melodies could be created using mathematical formulas. He soon discovered that this theory was not sound. In fact, the more he studied, the more he realized that true lyrical and musical inspiration came when observation, experience, and knowledge are combined in a creative method. As Lowry had always used those three elements in writing his sermons, he discovered that if he tossed out math, his transition to music was an easy one. In fact, when he drew from the elements that had provided the inspiration for his spellbinding sermons, he found he could write songs that contained both spiritual and physical value.

Once he immersed himself in composing, Lowry wrote such Christian classics as "Shall We Gather at the River?" "I Need Thee Every Hour," "All the Way My Savior Leads Me," and "We're Marching to Zion." With their positive messages and upbeat melodies, these songs quickly found favor with audiences around the world. In fact, the genius in Lowry's work brought scores of men and women to his door inquiring as to his methods for composing.

"I have no method," he would tell them. "Sometimes the music comes and the words follow, fitted insensibly to the melody. I watch my moods, and when anything good strikes me, whether words or music, and no matter where I am, at home or on the street, I jot it down. Often the margin of a newspaper or the back of an envelope serves as a notebook. My brain is a sort of spinning machine, I think, for there is music running through it all the time. I do not pick out my music on the keys of an instrument. The tunes of nearly all the hymns I have written have been completed on paper before I tried them on the organ. Frequently the words of the hymn and the music have been written at the same time."

One of these special moments happened during the Easter season of 1874. Contemplating the meaning of Christ's death and resurrection, Lowry read Luke 24:6–7: "He is not here, but is risen: remember how he spake unto you when he was yet in Galilee, saying, The Son of man must be delivered into the hands of sinful men, and be crucified, and the third day rise again." As he considered these two verses, the story of Easter became vividly clear. Lowry picked up a pen and began to jot down his inspiration in verse form. While on the surface the lyrics of his short poem seemed simple, the actual message in the two-line stanzas was deeply profound, the product of decades of Bible study.

The verses were foreboding and steeped in hopelessness. They were mournful and dark, reflecting emotions of deep loss. Yet the chorus that completed the trio of verses was incredibly upbeat and hopeful. The word that anchored this change in mood was *arose*, a word commonly used during this time to describe a person being pulled up after baptism by immersion. Many would say, "They arose out of the water a new person."

With this thought in mind, Lowry used "arose" as the key to the song's message but changed it from out of the water to out of the grave. Lowry used the word *triumph* to emphasize Christ's victory over death. For Lowry triumph also represented the change a person underwent when giving his or her heart to Christ. Suddenly they were conquerors, and nothing could defeat them, not even those who lived with Satan in the "dark domain."

When Lowry matched a melody to the somber verses, the strains were dark and the tempo slow. Yet when the good news of a risen Savior was revealed in the chorus, suddenly the music was bright and uplifting. It was as if a celebration had broken out in the midst of a wake. Essentially, this hymn contains all the elements of a New Orleans Dixieland funeral. On the way to the grave, the music is slow and mournful, but on the return the instruments play songs that are uplifting and joyous. Thus, Lowry's "Christ Arose" might well be considered the first Dixieland jazz piece.

An immediate hit in churches when it was first published, this Easter song remains popular almost a century and a half later. This is partly because it is easy to sing. Yet, in truth, it is the genius of the lyrical message found in "Christ Arose" that makes it so timeless. This hymn paints as vivid a picture as any Lowry sermon, but does it so simply that anyone can understand it. It also tells the whole story of the cross, beginning with Good Friday, but not ending until the triumphant victory over the tomb. While so many hymns have lyrics that can be sung without feeling, this one embraces emotion. And although Robert Lowry's best-remembered message was also his shortest, it remains an essential facet of Easter because it trumpets the good news of that day: "Christ arose!"

The Tradition of Easter Parades

The Bible records two parades the first Passion Week. The first took place on Palm Sunday as Jesus was welcomed to Jerusalem by an adoring throng. This crowd saw him as the man who would free them from Roman rule while restoring their long-lost kingdom. This was a jubilant occasion, but the triumph of that day would soon be forgotten, replaced by a vindictive mob chanting for blood.

The second parade was later in the week. This event was also watched by a large crowd. Again Jesus was the focal point. Yet instead of cheering, now the crowd ridiculed and derided the "King of the Jews." As he carried a cross to the hill where he would be executed, Jesus suffered from the worst human behavior. People lashed out and spat on him. He was cursed and reviled. For those who followed Jesus, this was now the darkest moment in history. So much had changed in the days between these two parades.

In the information era, parades are too old fashioned for most people, so the few that remain are giddy and light. Even

with their bunnies and brightly colored floats, these parades are often viewed like carnivals and Sunday picnics: relics of the past. Though it is hard for many today to believe, parades were once a vital facet of Christian worship and Easter.

During the Dark Ages, in many parts of Eastern Europe, church members would gather on Easter Sunday in a designated spot before church. In some cases that might have been in a field or graveyard where sunrise services were held. Other groups would meet on the edge of town. Then the congregation would solemnly walk to the church for services. In some places, the congregation would form another parade after the morning services, retracing their steps while singing songs of praise.

Even in the Dark Ages, those who participated in parades wore their finest clothing. When they appeared in public to honor Christ, they felt they needed to look their best. This display of new attire showed the members' respect for their heavenly King. Therefore parades had a fresh look that was rarely seen in these bleak times.

These early parades had two purposes. The first was to provide a lesson to the church members in the unity of spirit found in true faith. Therefore, through the solemn beginnings to the joyful endings of the parades, Christians could fully realize and appreciate the entire events of the first Easter weekend. The second objective of the parade was to alert those in the community who did not attend church of what they were missing. The parades, with their prayers and singing, presented a human example of the faith that brought people together and made them stronger. Thus, these early parades were missionary tools for churches, a way to reach lost souls in a highly visible manner. By coming out from behind the walls of the sanctuary and walking down city streets, these parades allowed the church to

take the message of Christ to those who would otherwise not have the opportunity to hear it. In the Middle Ages the clergy began to expand the concept of parades into a teaching tool. In the week before Easter, paintings and statues would be placed along city streets. Church members would walk from the first to the second statue and continue until they had seen all the displays or stations. The stations of the cross parades were intended to present the entire Easter story. As they became popular, the parades were expanded from just a few stops to fourteen, always beginning with Christ's being condemned to death by Pilate. The stations that followed included Jesus having the cross laid on his shoulder, Jesus falling, Jesus seeing his mother, Simon of Cyrene being made to bear the cross, Christ's face being wiped, Christ falling again, Christ meeting the women of Jerusalem, Christ falling for a third time, Christ being stripped, Christ being nailed to the cross, Christ dying, his body being removed from the cross, and — the most important and final station — Christ being taken to the tomb where he rises from the grave.

To a public that had no access to a Bible and often could not understand the language in which services were conducted, these displays helped them understand their faith and connect with it in a very personal way. In fact, the stations of the cross parades were probably one of the first practices of what has become a common modern witnessing tool: handing out tracts. It is certain these parades led many lost souls to churches.

When Lent was expanded to forty days, parades were incorporated on the most special days of this period. The most famous of these was Mardi Gras. Today's wild Mardi Gras parades are much different than the original, more religious events of the Middle Ages. Nevertheless, even though most church leaders

would like to dismiss the connection, Mardi Gras parades have a tie to church practices of the past. While in this case all the religious aspects of the parade have been lost, in many nations a dramatic form of the stations of the cross remains true to the historical record and very popular.

In many Latin American and European nations, Easter parades remain a solemn and moving experience. Instead of using paintings or statues to represent the stations of Christ's final walk, the events now unfold with members of the community playing all the roles. The man chosen to portray Jesus considers the part as a great opportunity to experience some of the pain and agony of the original trip from judgment to crucifixion. And while no one today is nailed to the cross, the lead actor is nevertheless lashed to the wood and displayed as Christ was two thousand years ago. These powerful parades draw huge crowds and are seen as important reminders of the real reason behind Easter.

Though they are not as popular as other holiday parades, a few American cities still welcome spring with an Easter parade. These are rarely religious in nature and usually embrace only the secular symbols of the season, such as bunnies and colored eggs. Yet in the days just after the end of World War II, these spring parades were popular enough to rate a musical treatment by Hollywood.

In 1948, Judy Garland starred in MGM's blockbuster *Easter Parade*. In the movie Judy wrapped her magnificent voice around songs penned by legendary tunesmith Irving Berlin. Hits from the motion picture included "Happy Easter" and the title cut "Easter Parade." With its Technicolor photography and solid cast, the film was a box-office smash and remains entertaining today. Yet it had no link to the religious reasons for the holiday.

Today few American churches use parades as a part of their worship. In fact, in these times of separation of church and state, most cities have even given up the practice of Easter parades. Yet Christ has not been totally removed from Easter celebrations, as proven by the great success of the recent movie *The Passion of the Christ*. Like *Easter Parade*, this new film was a box-office hit. Yet while the first Easter movie was all fluff, *The Passion of the Christ* was taken directly from the gospels, so it is a hard-hitting look at the events of Christ's last week on earth. It presents Jesus' final walk — from judgment to the cross — in greater detail than could have been imagined by those who had created the stations of the cross parades. Surprising many, the film's stark portrayal of the first Easter helped produce a new interest in the life of Christ. Hence, *The Passion of the Christ* clearly showed that people were still ready to view and consider the real events of the first Easter.

Perhaps because of this fresh look at the resurrection, church congregations might begin to again use Easter parades as their forebears did. Perhaps now is the time for congregations to joyfully march through the streets of their cities and towns singing anthems of resurrection and praising the Lord for the eternal gift he has given them. Even in the information age, this kind of Easter parade might well be the greatest tool in reminding thousands of why that first Easter Sunday remains an event that can forever change lives today.

At Calvary

*O*ne sunny Chicago morning in 1895, William R. Newell was lost in thought. The noted preacher, who also taught at the city's Moody Bible Institute, walked robotically toward his classroom, his mind consumed by images of Jesus' last hours on earth. Those mental pictures always took Newell to Calvary—"the place of the skull." As the world around him faded, a picture of Christ being nailed to the cross came into sharp, clear focus. Suddenly this vision was so strong Newell felt as if he were actually viewing the crucifixion. It was as if he were there to watch his Savior die at Calvary. In his entire life, never had this facet of Jesus' life seemed so real.

Rather than try to shake the horrific image from his head, Newell forgot about the time and his scheduled teaching assignment and stole away to an empty classroom. Closing the door, he sat down at a student's desk to pray. As he immersed himself in prayer, the only sounds he heard were the ticking of a clock and the muffled voices of students coming from beyond the door.

As he often did when consumed by spiritual questions, when he finished praying, Newell pulled out a pencil and paper to jot down the images imprinted in his brain. As he began to write,

the horror of Christ's death was soon replaced by the compelling thought of the hopelessness of human life without this sacrifice. It was grace, he thought, which had saved him. As he centered his thoughts on grace, he also considered Paul's writings in 1 Corinthians 1:18: "For the preaching of the cross is to them that perish foolishness; but unto us which are saved it is the power of God."

To put these different thoughts into perspective, Newell considered his own conversion and what it had meant to his life. He recalled his younger days spent living a worldly existence, not knowing the measure of grace that stood within his reach and not understanding the meaning of Christ's life, death, and resurrection. He then contrasted those days to his life as a Christian, a pastor, and a teacher. Even as he tried to understand these separate elements of his own history, Newell found himself always taken back to the image of Christ at Calvary.

Consumed by thoughts of random events separated by almost nineteen hundred years, he began to scribble down stanzas of poetry. In just a few minutes, and with hardly any effort, Newell wrote his personal view of salvation. As he put the final words on paper, his mind quickly cleared, and he felt a huge burden lifted from his shoulders. Now realizing his students would be waiting for him, Newell got up from the desk and hurried out into the hallway.

This professor's untitled poem might have been forgotten, set aside, or used as an outline for a future sermon at the Bethesda Congregational Church had Daniel Towner not been walking by as William Newell stepped into the hallway. Seeing his friend, Newell waved as if asking Towner to stop.

Daniel Towner was an imposing figure with an unruly crop of dark hair and a mustache that all but covered his top lip. If

he had been wearing a flannel shirt, people might have thought him to be a lumberjack or farmer. But dressed in a black suit, as he was now, he appeared to be a rich oil tycoon. In truth he was none of those things.

Towner was born in Rome, Pennsylvania, in 1850. Blessed with a beautiful baritone voice and an aptitude for composition and arrangement, he studied music first with his father and later in private lessons. At the age of twenty, when many men were just beginning to sing in a choir, he became the music director of the Centenary Methodist Episcopal Church in Binghamton, New York. Twenty-three years later, Towner had relocated to Ohio, when in 1893, Dwight L. Moody noticed him during an evangelistic crusade. Impressed with Towner's voice and abilities as an arranger, the evangelist convinced the now middle-aged choir director to move to Chicago and head the music department at the Moody Bible Institute. This new position gave Towner the freedom and time for musical creation, leading to Towner's penning hundreds of songs, including "Redeemed," "Grace Greater Than Our Sins," and "Trust and Obey." At Moody he also edited some of the bestselling hymnals of the day.

On the morning when Newell spotted Towner in the hallway, the latter had no clue he would soon be composing the music for what would become one of the most moving Christian songs of all time. Even as Newell worked his way across the crowded hall and cornered the music director, Towner could not have guessed what the professor wanted.

With the sound of students' voices echoing off the walls coupled to the drone of leather-soled shoes marching along the wooden floor in the background, Newell yanked out his poem and pushed it at Towner. Over the noise, he explained that this

At Calvary

Years I spent in vanity and pride,
Caring not my Lord was crucified,
Knowing not it was for me he died
On Calvary.

By God's Word at last my sin I learned;
Then I trembled at the law I'd spurned,
Till my guilty soul imploring turned
To Calvary.

Now I've giv'n to Jesus ev'rything;
Now I gladly own him as my King;
Now my ransomed soul can only sing
Of Calvary.

Oh, the love that drew salvation's plan!
Oh, the grace that brought it down to man!
Oh, the mighty gulf that God did span
At Calvary.

Refrain
Mercy there was great, and grace was free;
Pardon there was multiplied to me;
There my burdened soul found liberty,
At Calvary.

was something he had just written that might work as a song. He then asked Towner if he would study it and try to compose a melody to go with the poem.

As Newell rushed to his class, Towner leaned up against a wall and read the hastily written words. He knew Newell well from his sermons. At times you had to be an intellectual just to understand him. Usually the professor's writings were intricate, detailed, and filled with intellectual theology and complex sentence structure. Yet this poem was none of that. It was simple, direct, and personal.

Towner walked quickly to his office, sat down at his piano, and reread the verses several more times. As he did, a melody began to play in his head. It had a gospel feel, much like a Southern folk song, and even though it dealt with Christ's suffering on the cross, the music cried to be set free, to float in a manner that lifted the listener toward heaven. As he wrote down what he was hearing in his head, Towner was somewhat surprised by the simplicity of his latest creation. The melody contained only three chords. And though he felt it fit Newell's words perfectly, he wondered if the dynamic, deep-thinking theologian might feel let down by the music's elementary nature.

After finishing his class, Newell made his way to Towner's office. He was hoping Towner would have at least started thinking about a tune for his poem, and he was shocked to find that Towner had not only started but had already finished writing it. Towner, still unsure, played the song through once, watching for Newell's reaction. What Towner saw on the professor's face proved Newell also believed the music matched his words. Without discussion, both men then sat on the piano bench and sang "At Calvary" for the first time.

Most songs are written and lost. They never find publishers and are rarely heard by audiences. They remain undiscovered until they are eventually forgotten by their composers. If Newell had still been preaching in the east and Towner had remained a music director in a Cincinnati church, their song would never have been made or published. But because they worked for Dwight L. Moody, they had the powerful resources of his organization surrounding them. Therefore "At Calvary" was immediately published. Then, through Moody's nationwide crusades, thousands heard it.

While many of the hymns trumpeted by the Moody Bible Institute found great initial popularity and then faded, "At Calvary" did not. Perhaps this was because it was not a corporate church song; it was a personal testimony. It was Newell's own profound salvation experience put into words so universal that every believer could relate to them. That testimony was also matched to music that anyone could sing.

Though not intended to be an Easter song, the imagery found in "At Calvary" naturally coupled the hymn to worship services reflecting on the cross and the resurrection. It has therefore emerged as a well-known and beloved Easter standard.

After composing his song of faith, William Newell lived another fifty-one years. During this time he wrote thousands of words and gave hundreds of sermons centered on explaining the meaning of grace. He usually presented grace in this manner: "The discovery by the creature that he is truly the object of Divine grace, works the utmost humility: for the receiver of grace is brought to know his own absolute unworthiness, and his complete inability to attain worthiness: yet he finds himself blessed—on another principle, outside of himself!" These complex thoughts on grace were surely in his head as Newell

wrote his most remembered work. This is probably the kind of writing Towner expected when he was initially handed Newell's poem.

Yet while Newell's theological explanation of grace might have been great oratory, it was his simple hymn that best defined the way humans understood grace. Through this straightforward song, millions have come to fully understand why what happened at Calvary remains so important even today.

18

Blessed Redeemer

*I*n 1905 America was a nation with boundless energy and an optimistic spirit. The industrial age was making the United States one of the world's economic powers. American culture was being exported; in Europe people were flocking to Wild West shows and Tin Pan Alley musical shows. For many around the globe, America surely seemed like the land of opportunity. It was a place that welcomed new people and new ideas. It was a country where even immigrants were given a chance at achieving the American dream, and millions were flocking to Ellis Island to try to realize that dream.

With the dawn of this new age, electricity spread across the nation like a windblown wildfire. Millions now could pick up a phone in their homes and be connected to others thousands of miles away. The Wright brothers managed to glide into the era of flight, and people like Henry Ford were developing con traptions that would soon replace the horse. This was an age of transition and growth, and Chicago was at the center of it. In fact, the Windy City was one of the most exciting places on earth, a city where change seemed to move at light speed. It was also one of the religious centers of America, enriching the

lives of millions around the globe through its exports of evangelists, song leaders, books, and music.

With the hustle and bustle of this new era all around them, about the only place Chicagoans could retreat was one of the city's thousands of churches. Houses of worship offered a chance to escape the frenetic pace and continual reverberation of the industrial age. These gathering places provided an atmosphere of peace and understanding. They were unchanging anchors in the midst of the confusion of the modern age. Yet they were more than havens of solitude; they were also inspirational places. And, in an increasingly impersonal world, the church was the place that most recognized the potential found in each individual's God-given talents.

On a Sunday morning in 1905, a bright little girl named Avis joined her family in a pew at the city's Moody Church. Just ten, Avis loved church services because she so enjoyed the musical part of worship. She loved to sing, and she usually sang at the top of her lungs. Yet this day it was not the familiar songs that stuck in her mind. On this Sunday she was drawn to the voice of a young teenager who sang a song he had written. She was so impressed with young Harry Loes's original musical offering that she felt inspired to compose her own song that afternoon. Soon, she and Loes were both performing original works for Sunday school and church. Yet at that time neither would have guessed they would someday come together to create one of the most beloved Easter songs in music history.

The Moody Church was a part of the Moody Bible Institute. The latter was the birthplace of many of America's most beloved hymns, where Dwight Moody sought out the greatest talents in the fields of music and speaking and brought them to the Windy City to instruct the next generation of Christian

Blessed Redeemer

Up Calvary's mountain, one dreadful morn,
Walked Christ my Savior, weary and worn;
Facing for sinners death on the cross,
That he might save them from endless loss.

"Father forgive them!" thus did he pray,
E'en while his lifeblood flowed fast away;
Praying for sinners while in such woe
No one but Jesus ever loved so.

O how I love him, Savior and Friend,
How can my praises ever find end!
Through years unnumbered on heaven's shore,
My tongue shall praise him forevermore.

Refrain
Blessed Redeemer! Precious Redeemer!
Seems now I see him on Calvary's tree;
Wounded and bleeding, for sinners pleading,
Blind and unheeding—dying for me!

singers and preachers. So it was only natural that some of these great talents were not only inspired by the atmosphere at the school, but by each other. Such was the case with the writing of "Blessed Redeemer."

Harry Dixon Loes was affiliated with the Moody Institute for most of his life. Even before he came to teach music at the school, he visited the campus and consulted with some of the teachers about songs he had written. Loes also sat in on sermons and lectures, using what he gleaned from these as inspiration for his own songs. In 1920, twenty-eight-year-old Loes was taken by a sermon he heard at Moody on the subject of Christ dying for the sins of man. In fact, Loes was so moved he felt a call to use this as a theme for a new gospel song.

Before staring to write, Loes considered the price Jesus paid on the cross. He was a student of history, so he knew well the painful agony that was a part of crucifixion. The writer fully understood that the suffering of those executed this way was unimaginable. That Jesus could have walked away from this fate made his dying on the cross much more powerful for Loes. "He didn't have to do it," Loes later explained to his students. "Christ was not forced to die for us; he *chose* to die for us." To Loes, that choosing made the events that began on a dark Friday more than just another in a long line of public executions. Because of his choice, Jesus' dying on the cross became the most important and blessed milestone in the history of the world.

Once this theme became clear in his mind, Loes picked up a pen and quickly scribbled his basic melody. Even as he wrote the final bars of the verse, he sensed his latest work was not complete. He knew that "Blessed Redeemer" would not reach its full potential nor would its message be fully realized until lyrics echoed the passion of his music. Yet, for reasons known

only to him, Loes did not choose to compose the words himself. Loes knew many gifted writers. In fact, scores of them could be found all around him at Moody. Yet he passed over these men and instead turned to the talents of a woman he had known at Moody Church since his youth.

Born in 1895, Avis Burgeson Christiansen lived her whole life in Chicago, Illinois. Though just twenty-five in 1920, she was already known as one of the best hymn writers in the Midwest. As a writer she usually composed both lyrics and music, but as she had come to work more closely with Loes, she had expanded her vision to include arrangements for some of his music and lyrics for his melodies. So she was hardly surprised when he asked her to take a look at his "Blessed Redeemer."

Like Loes, Christiansen often contemplated the events of Good Friday. The stark images that filled her mind when she imagined the crucifixion would have normally depressed her. She simply could not bear the horror of that event. As a mother, she grew even more depressed when she considered the emotions that Mary must have felt that day. Yet Loes's music took her beyond the bleak images of Good Friday. It presented her with the wonderful reason Christ had chosen to pay that incredible price. As she listened to the melody, Christiansen fully sensed the power and glory of the resurrection. She also realized the full freedom of knowing her own sins were completely forgiven. So, even though the resurrection is not mentioned in her lyrics, forgiveness for humankind is at the heart of "Blessed Redeemer." It is a hymn of great hope.

Christiansen kept her words as simple and direct as Loes's melody. There was nothing fancy or dynamic in the woman's verses, but there was a feeling of power and glory that echoed each time the chorus was sung. In a sense, both the words

and music were understated and thus all the more powerful. Loes was thrilled with Christiansen's contribution to "Blessed Redeemer." He now knew it was complete.

"Blessed Redeemer" was first published the same year it was written. Within a generation it became one of the most widely used songs in church hymnals. With its lyrics centering upon the events of the crucifixion, "Blessed Redeemer" was definitely an Easter song, forever linked to Good Friday services. Yet it was more too. Because of its message of sacrifice, forgiveness, and hope, it was also an invitation call that offered safe passage beyond the cross and into eternity.

This hymn would not have been written if it hadn't been for a church that encouraged its youth to take part in services as well as to tell their stories in song. That is the reason Harry Dixon Loes met Avis Burgeson Christiansen. Without that meeting there surely would have been no "Blessed Redeemer," and the Easter season would not have one of its most powerful hymns.

*O*ne Day

*J*ohn Wilbur Chapman was born in Richmond, Indiana, on June 17, 1859. Raised in a devout Christian family, Chapman never remembered a time when Christ was not an important factor in the decisions he made in his life. Still, even with this knowledge, he did not publicly acknowledge his faith until he was seventeen years old. Though the congregation celebrated with the Chapman family that day, none could have predicted the great things that were in this young man's future.

Soon after Chapman accepted Christ as his Savior, he came forward again to give his life to Christian service as a pastor. His focus on this lifetime commitment would never sway. After diligent study in college and seminary, he led churches in Albany, New York, Philadelphia, Pennsylvania, and New York City. A dynamic speaker with a gentle touch and a ready ear, he probably would have continued successfully in this role if not for a trip to the Chicago World's Fair in 1893.

During the last half of the eighteenth century, Chicago was a place exploding with enthusiasm and wanted to show off its many accomplishments and opportunities through the fair. To make sure everything was presented in a first-class fashion,

the city employed 44,000 workers and spent twenty-eight million dollars to build the 633-acre lakefront fairground. It was a marvel of such scope that thousands paid a quarter every day just to tour the site as it was being constructed. On May 1, one hundred thousand people were on hand to watch President Grover Cleveland touch a switch, setting the generators that ran the 65,000 exhibits and hundreds of restaurants in motion. This fair was where many of the twenty-seven million visitors first tasted ice cream, hamburgers, and carbonated soda. One of those to take in all the sights was John Chapman, but he was not there as a guest; he was a participant.

The New York City preacher had been invited by the Windy City's own Reverend Dwight L. Moody to be a part of a huge revival. While speaking in front of thousands at the fair, Chapman felt called to change the direction of his ministry. When he shared his vision, Moody and other evangelists encouraged Chapman to hit the revival circuit. They explained that he could take the message of salvation to more people in a week this way than he could reach in a year from his pulpit. Chapman was tempted but held back until he attended a meeting at the Bible Conference and Chautauqua Center in Winona Lake, Indiana. Here Chapman saw thousands of young people coming together with the sole intent of working for the cause of Christ. Seized by the power he witnessed at Winona Lake, Chapman left the pulpit and hit the road, leading crusades while also developing new Bible conference centers in Montreat, North Carolina, and Stony Brook, Long Island, New York. His life was now completely consumed with passion for reaching the lost. Every plan he made was geared toward reaching this goal.

Two years after the closing of the world's fair, a wealthy Presbyterian layman, John H. Converse, heard Chapman preach.

One Day

One day when heaven was filled with his praises,
One day when sin was as black as could be,
Jesus came forth to be born of a virgin
Dwelt among men, my example is he!

One day they led him up Calvary's mountain,
One day they nailed him to die on the tree,
Suffering anguish, despised and rejected;
Bearing our sins, my Redeemer is he!

One day they left him alone in the garden,
One day he rested, from suffering free;
Angels came down over his tomb to keep vigil;
Hope of the hopeless my Savior is he!

One day the grave could conceal him no longer,
One day the stone rolled away from the door;
Then he arose, over death he had conquered;
Now is ascended, my Lord evermore!

One day the trumpet will sound for his coming,
One day the skies with his glory will shine;
Wonderful day, my beloved ones bringing;
Glorious Savior, this Jesus is mine!

Refrain
Living, he loved me; dying, he saved me;
Buried, he carried my sins far away;
Rising, he justified freely forever:
One day he's coming, oh, glorious day!

Converse was so impressed with the power of the evangelist's message that he set up a trust fund to underwrite the cost of all Chapman's programs. This was the ticket Chapman needed to take his vision to the world.

With solid financial backing, Chapman sought out Charles Alexander, one of the world's most renowned Christian vocalists. Over the next few years the duo led huge revivals in most major American cities as well as in Melbourne, Sydney, Manila, Hong Kong, Shanghai, Seoul, and Tokyo. Everywhere they went, thousands were converted to Christianity. Even for a man with Chapman's vision, the power he now saw in the message of Christ was almost overwhelming.

After returning from one of the tours, Chapman realized that everything he had been called to do, as well as all the decisions he had seen made for Christ, were because of just one day in human history — the day Jesus rose from the grave. The realization of how dramatically the first Easter had changed the world staggered the middle-aged man. Long before Hollywood happened upon the idea, Chapman suddenly recognized that this was "the greatest story ever told." Now, even with all of his success, he wondered if he was really doing an adequate job sharing that story with the lost masses. Was there a way he could take the message to even more people?

While at the Bible Conference Center in Stony Brook, Chapman began to restudy the book of Luke. What he read gave him the inspiration for an Easter song that is still being sung a century later. Thinking of the manger, the cross, and the resurrection, the evangelist began to write a sermon from what he had just read in Luke, but as he put pen to paper, a poem emerged. The verses Chapman composed in that sitting provide a complete biography of Christ from birth to the cross and beyond.

Though the poem had all the needed elements of a good message, being simple and powerful, Chapman felt it was somehow incomplete. Hence, he didn't want to share it with anyone in its current state.

In 1905, the evangelist had heard a high school student play a rousing gospel anthem on the piano and had been so impressed by this performance that he later spent time with the young man and his parents. Discovering that Charles Marsh was about to graduate, Chapman offered him a job with his organization. The boy eagerly took it, and three years later Marsh was arranging and playing the music featured at Chapman's crusades.

Thinking of Marsh, Chapman suddenly realized he had not written a message or a poem; rather, he had begun writing a song. Now he needed another member of his team to finish it. With the verses in hand, he rushed out to find Marsh. After he read "One Day" to the twenty-one-year-old musician, he left Marsh alone to complete the project.

Marsh had worked with Chapman long enough to know the man's taste in music. The pianist also understood the style of music needed for the evangelistic meetings, and he knew that the melody had to be easy to learn and sing. With these thoughts in mind, Marsh sat down and composed a melody to go with the poem. He then took his finished work back to Chapman and played the new music. Chapman was thrilled by what he heard.

A few nights later "One Day" premiered in front of an enthusiastic revival crowd. The response was overwhelming. Audiences requested it night after night. The Chapman-Marsh hymn quickly became one of the organization's most beloved anthems, but for four years it was also the only place the song

could be heard. This powerful musical biography of the life of Jesus Christ was not published until 1911. When it finally did find its way into a hymnal, "One Day" quickly became one of the most popular gospel songs in the nation.

For the final decade of his life, "One Day" served as John Chapman's theme. As a man completely committed to living out the Great Commission, the evangelist felt the lyrics told the essence of Christian faith better than any sermon he had ever written. In 1918, on Christmas day — the very day that inspired the first verse of his "One Day" — Chapman died. But that was not the end of the story. Thanks to the promise found in the fourth verse of his hymn, the evangelist's second life was just beginning. Easter is the one day John Chapman wanted the world to never forget, and thanks in part to his hymn, it never will.

20

The Custom of
Dressing Up for Easter

For generations, Christians have dressed up in their finest garments for Easter. This tradition has been the subject of paintings, photographs, magazine stories, news features, and even motion pictures. How dressing up for Easter began is rooted in many different holiday practices. Because facets of dressing up originated in so many different times and places, today few know anything about the custom's humble beginnings.

There are several reasons the custom of dressing up for Easter came to the forefront of the holiday. Surprisingly, none of these reasons were initiated by merchants or tailors. In fact, the tradition of wearing one's finest on Easter has three roots. The first is deeply embedded in the season when the holiday is celebrated, the second is related to events held in conjunction with Easter, and the last is entwined with the respect of commoners for royalty.

Easter was initially born from two distinct holiday celebrations. The first is Passover. During this ancient holiday steeped in Old Testament traditions and history, Jewish men and women

often wore their best clothing to the feast of the Passover. As early Jewish Christians often combined Passover with Easter, many of these new believers wore their finest to church services as well as to the Passover feast.

The second holiday forerunner to Easter and another element of the custom of dressing up for Easter comes from pagan customs. In many cultures spring was welcomed with huge celebrations. In the minds of people who had just survived another tough winter, this was a time to be thankful that the dark, cold days had passed and the days of brightness and sunshine had reappeared. Tradition had it that new clothes were to be worn at these celebrations as a way of welcoming the hope and new life that came with warmer days. When people from these cultures became Christians, missionaries gave them a new reason to dress up during the spring. This time of putting on one's finest was a way of acknowledging the new life that came through being reborn in Christ. Thus, wearing new clothing during the Easter weekend was a way of displaying one's new faith.

The idea that new clothing was essential during Easter day services can also be traced to two other early Christian Easter customs. In many churches babies were baptized or dedicated only on Easter Sunday. As this was seen as the most important day in a child's life, the little one wore a new outfit that had either been sewn or purchased just for this occasion. Most baptismal clothing was seen as being so special it was worn only once, then set aside and kept as a memento. Over time, the families who brought their babies forward also began to wear new clothing on this day. Thus, baptisms on Easter Sunday created a need for special clothing for new parents and their children.

Another ancient European Easter custom involved weddings. Many churches adopted the practice of conducting marriage services on Easter Sunday. Naturally the bride and groom, as well as their families, felt a need to look their best at the weddings. So they dressed up in their finest for the ceremony, which was a part of the Easter service. Both baptisms and weddings provided a strong reason for dressing up at Easter, but there was another tradition that might have even been a stronger motive for many to dress in their finest on the holiday. This tradition was tied to a common person's relationship with royalty.

In the Dark and Middle Ages, few peasants were ever invited to the castles of noblemen. If an audience was requested, then the guests felt it was essential to look their best when entering the home of the ruling family. Thus special care was taken while getting ready for this audience. Even the clergy put on their finest robes before going to a royal appointment. For many this social custom carried over to worship practices. Many church members felt a need to dress up each Sunday simply because they were going to God's house. In the minds of these Christians, the Lord was the King of Kings. Thus, they believed they should wear their best for him each Sunday. Because Easter was the holiest of all days, it required a Christian to wear something very special to honor Christ. Many fulfilled this custom by either sewing very fancy clothing for the day or purchasing the nicest suit or dress they could afford.

Over time, dressing up became more than simply an Easter custom; it turned into a kind of competition. Church members would check out what others were wearing and compare those outfits to their own. Hence, the sin of envy sometimes crept into Easter worship services. Yet even with this negative emotional response causing some to miss the reason for celebrating

Easter, the clergy did not discourage the practice of wearing fine clothing. In fact, many priests had special robes sewn for the holiday services.

In the late Middle Ages, one's social status became even more important. Thus, for many, the need to "outdress" others in church took on a sense of urgency. If someone else had finer clothing than your family did, it placed that family at a higher social level. Thus appearances meant everything to some people, even during Easter worship.

Children usually despised this fashion struggle. Yet while they often disliked having to wear fancy garments to church, they did manage to find a good use for hats and bonnets. These items came off children's heads as soon as they began their Easter egg hunts. Often hats and bonnets were employed in gathering up all the hidden brightly colored treasures.

After the Reformation, many denominations frowned upon anything they saw as frivolous. Because Puritans and other conservative groups banned all the elements of Christmas and Easter, as well as any outward or spontaneous emotions in church services, extravagant clothing went the way of colored eggs and Christmas presents. Because of this stark view of faith, no one dressed up for the holidays in America or Britain for several hundred years.

In the mid-1800s, Easter made a comeback. During this time most Protestant churches modified their doctrines to allow congregations to once again celebrate traditional church holidays. Thus the old custom of wearing new clothing to honor Easter returned to the Christian fashion scene. Initially the revival of this tradition was most obvious in the bonnets women either bought or made for the holidays. These hats were not simple little head toppers; they were brightly colored fashion statements

sporting ribbons, flowers, feathers, and pins. The bonnets were so elaborate that many churches actually held contests, choosing the finest hats worn to the service each year. Some women spent months working on their Easter headgear.

Another tradition renewed with this reawakening of Easter was parading down a community's main street after church services. In the early part of the last century it was so common for church groups to take part in these parades that many towns blocked off routes for the marchers. In New York City, thousands of people annually strolled down Fifth Avenue in the Sunday Easter parade. The purpose of this walk was simply to show off their new clothes. Similarly, in thousands of towns and cities across the United States and Europe, Easter became one of the few times when members of all of a community's different churches would come together for one purpose. Even if these parades were really more fashion statements than professions of faith, they still served at least as a casual reminder of the reason for being in a worship service on this special day.

The Easter fashion parades in the early twentieth century finally gave merchants a marketing angle they had never been able to find in this spring holiday. With clothing now having become such an obviously important holiday element, Easter clothing sales exploded. For the very first time in the modern age, shops took great concern in supplying Christians with the proper attire needed to celebrate Easter. In fact this marketing plan was so successful that for several generations the mentality of needing a new outfit for Easter fueled a large part of spring clothing sales.

Today Easter hats and bonnets have been all but forgotten. In fact, few believe that it's necessary to dress up in something new for worship at Easter. So the spring clothing push at stores

is now rarely seen. In some ways this is probably good. So much of the fashion statements made during past spring holiday seasons were about competition and vanity, not faith and worship. Yet in today's casual world, it might be good to occasionally put on the finest in order to honor the one who was stripped bare and crucified for man's sins. If placed in that perspective, the tradition of dressing up for Easter could continue with the focus on showing honor and respect for the King who laid down his life so all his subjects could inherit his kingdom. That is a reason to dress up on any day, but especially at Easter.

21

The Old Rugged Cross

The most powerful Easter symbol, the one that resounds most strongly with a majority of Christians, is the cross. The cross was where salvation began, where God's blood was shed for sinners, and where man tried unsuccessfully to put the Son of God to death. It is the reason there is an Easter and thus has become the most important image believers cling to as they think of their place in God's kingdom. Yet in spite of the true meaning of the cross and its unswerving marriage to Easter, the cross is used in many other ways too.

For centuries crosses have been everywhere. Thousands of families used the cross in their coat of arms. It was and is a fashion icon as millions wear crosses around their necks as jewelry. The cross can be found on church steeples as well as in stained-glass windows and at altars. It is on Bible covers and hymnals. You see it on shirts, hats, and even on silverware and glasses. Yet few people fully understand the cross's place in history or even its place in the Christian faith. A popular hymn, written more than eighteen hundred years after the crucifixion, helped fully illuminate the real nature of the cross to people around the globe.

There is a saying that all of us have a cross to bear. Certainly this was true in the case of George Bennard. Born in Iowa in 1873, George was a small, smart boy who was often picked on by the larger students in his school. Naturally, because of his diminutive stature, he was somewhat shy and far from physically strong. Due to both his brains and lack of brawn, it looked as though the lad would be best suited for bookkeeping or teaching. Though he had the native intelligence for both, he was cheated out of gaining enough education to enter either field, for in 1889, when his father suddenly passed away, Bennard's life took a tragic turn. The eldest of five children, Bennard was expected to run the farm that supported the family. Though it was a task he was ill equipped to handle, he did not shy away from the challenge. He labored from dawn to dusk without complaining about the work or the things he had been forced to give up. Yet though it seemed his greatest potential would be forever lost in the dust of the fields, a small evening church service gave him a sneak preview of some special opportunities that lay just down life's road.

Though still a teen, George was in a sense a mature man when he walked the aisle accepting Christ as his Savior during a Salvation Army revival. Besides coming to see Jesus in a new light, on this night he also felt a call to preach the gospel. Still needing to support his mother and sisters, George was unable to immediately respond to that call. Yet he made a pledge that was far from forgotten.

For some education is simple; for others it is a task that requires great discipline and sacrifice. Circumstances beyond his control forced Bennard into a position of learning through long hours of solitary study. Whenever he wasn't working, George had a book in his hands. He constantly pushed himself

The Old Rugged Cross

On a hill far away stood an old rugged cross,
The emblem of suffering and shame;
And I love that old cross where the dearest and best
For a world of lost sinners was slain.

O that old rugged cross, so despised by the world,
Has a wondrous attraction for me;
For the dear Lamb of God left his glory above
To bear it to dark Calvary.

In that old rugged cross, stained with blood so divine,
A wondrous beauty I see,
For 'twas on that old cross Jesus suffered and died,
To pardon and sanctify me.

To the old rugged cross I will ever be true;
Its shame and reproach gladly bear;
Then he'll call me some day to my home far away,
Where his glory forever I'll share.

Refrain
So I'll cherish the old rugged cross,
Till my trophies at last I lay down;
I will cling to the old rugged cross,
And exchange it some day for a crown.

to learn things a college education would have given him. This endeavor was difficult, but he would not give up.

After his siblings were all on their own and he had gotten married, Bennard felt it was time to finally and fully respond to his promise to serve God. Returning to the Salvation Army, he enlisted and became a solider for the Lord. Bennard's passion to help "the least of these" moved him quickly through the ranks of the organization. Within eight years he was in charge of a brigade and was overseeing large worship and charity mission programs. Eventually he felt a need to go beyond what he saw as the Salvation Army's limits, so he resigned his position and entered the ministry. After pastoring several churches through the Methodist Episcopal organization, he struck out on the evangelistic trail. With his sincere demeanor and passionate sermons, he was soon regularly traveling from his Michigan home to the East Coast. For the next few decades he was so much in demand he actually spent much more time on the road than he did at home.

On the eve of his fortieth birthday, Bennard had become one of the nation's most celebrated evangelists. Yet even after more than twenty years in the ministry and thousands of sermons, this American gospel giant was still confronting facets of his faith he couldn't fully comprehend. In his quest to continue to learn and grow, he was always searching for new ways of viewing Scripture. As the summer of 1912 slipped into autumn, this pursuit brought the cross into focus as more than a historical event or overused religious symbol. Suddenly Bennard saw it as a living vehicle of faith.

"I was praying for a full understanding of the cross and its plan in Christianity," he later told friends. "As I read and studied and prayed, I saw Christ and the cross inseparably. The scene

pictured a method, outlined a process, and revealed the consummation of spiritual experience. It was like seeing John 3:16 leave the printed page, take form, and act out the meaning of redemption. While watching this scene with my mind's eye, the theme of the song came to me, and with it the melody."

Seized by his new, deeper understanding of the meaning of the cross, Bennard tried to write down verses to his vision. Yet nothing concrete came to him. The words were lost in a mental fog, seemingly just out of reach. So he set his idea to the side and waited for the Lord to speak to him again. As he waited, Bennard held a series of revival meetings in Michigan then traveled to New York for several weeks to speak before large crowds there. At each stop he tried to write, but nothing inspired flowed from his pen. Even when he took a few days off and worked in the office of his Albion, Michigan, home, Bennard struck out. Yet toiling long hours as a teen on the farm and being forced to wait to pursue his own life and dreams had taught him great patience. Thus, when most people would have given up on these failed attempts at composing a song about the cross, Bennard kept trying.

"The more I contemplated these truths found in John 3:16," Bennard informed his close friends, "the more convinced I became that the cross was far more than just a religious symbol but rather the very heart of the gospel." Unable to fully convey this subject even in his sermons, he fought even harder to finish the song that seemed just out of reach. Thanksgiving and Christmas came and went, and the composition remained just as it had the first day it was conceived. Then, on December 29, as he began a revival at the Friend's Church in Sturgeon Bay, Wisconsin, inspiration struck again, though still the hymn did not instantly emerge from his mind in a completed form. In fact

it came to Bennard slowly, day by day. He did not finish the final verse until the last night of services on January 12, 1913.

After receiving help putting "The Old Rugged Cross" into manuscript form, Bennard mailed to it songwriter and musical publisher Charles H. Gabriel. Gabriel was one of the most talented composers in Christian music. He had been a part of creating such lasting gospel tributes as "The Way of the Cross," "Higher Ground," and "Send the Light." He had worked with some of the greatest songwriters in America, yet when he received this new hymn, even Gabriel was overwhelmed. He wrote to Bennard, "God has given you a song that will never die. It has moved us as no other song ever has moved us."

Published in 1915, "The Old Rugged Cross" quickly rivaled "Amazing Grace" as the world's most beloved hymn. Because it was inspired by George Bennard's view of the reality of the cross, the hymn has become an essential part of many Easter services. In his own quest to fully understand the greatest Christian symbol, Bennard brought the horror of the crucifixion, the perfection of Christ, and the beauty of salvation together in a hymn that will probably live forever. As no other song ever has, for millions, the "The Old Rugged Cross" has taken the symbol of the cross and made it real.

22

Living for Jesus

*F*or a Christian there is no irony in singing about living during the season when Christ's crucifixion is
recalled. Easter music can be joyful because it does not dwell
on the death of Jesus; rather, it celebrates the life found in a
resurrected Savior. The greatest story ever told does not end
with the cross or the grave; if it did then Easter would not be
celebrated at all. So each Easter season is about life.

On Easter in 1917, Carl Lowden reviewed a piece of music he
had written two years before. The idea of living for faith struck
a deep and resounding chord with the thirty-four-year-old
composer, and this vein of thought helped him generate one of
the world's most beloved hymns. Yet "Living for Jesus" proved
almost as difficult to write as it is for most people to actually
live completely for the Lord.

Lowden was born in Burlington, New Jersey, in 1883. His
father, an amateur musician, seemed intent on having his son
embrace music from an early age. To ensure this, the elder
Lowden often played a trumpet beside Carl's crib. His prayers
were answered as Carl began playing both piano and organ
before he learned to read. By his teens the youngster had mastered the violin, was conducting his church's orchestra, and

had even sold an original composition to the Hall-Mack Music Publishing Company. A few years later the young man's father was overcome with joy when Carl took a job at Hall-Mack.

After many successful years with the publisher, Lowden left the company to work as a musical editor for the Evangelical and Reformed Church. In 1917, he was assembling materials for a new songbook when he came across a hymn he had composed two years before. Lowden had hurriedly composed "Sunshine's Song" for a children's day service at his church. Hearing it performed proved to be a disappointment. While the tune was good, the writer felt the words were simply uninspired. Now, as he considered songs for a new hymnal, he took a second look at "Sunshine's Song." Though still recent, to Lowden the words read like something written a century before. While its theme and writing were too dated for a modern songbook, the tune's tempo and rhythm seemed too good to completely dismiss.

For several days Lowden worked on rewriting his original piece. His efforts provided nothing but fodder for the trash can. Each time he composed fresh lyrics, they were worse than the ones they were meant to replace. Eventually "Sunshine's Song" proved to be too frustrating to continue. Yet even as he turned his attention to other songs slated for the book, the tune kept playing in his head.

Sometime later Lowden found that he was now singing his children's song but with a new beginning lyric. He had no idea from where it had come, but he was now starting the verses with the line "living for Jesus." He also found that a chorus beginning with "Jesus Lord and Savior" had replaced the first part of the refrain. Even with this new, stronger theme cemented in his mind and ideas for lyrics seemingly appearing out of thin air, Lowden still could not finish rewriting "Sunshine's Song."

Living for Jesus

Living for Jesus, a life that is true,
Striving to please him in all that I do;
Yielding allegiance, glad hearted and free,
This is the pathway of blessing for me.

Living for Jesus who died in my place,
Bearing on Calvary my sin and disgrace;
Such love constrains me to answer his call,
Follow his leading and give him my all.

Living for Jesus, wherever I am,
Doing each duty in his holy name;
Willing to suffer affliction and loss,
Deeming each trial a part of my cross.

Living for Jesus through earth's little while,
My dearest treasure, the light of his smile;
Seeking the lost ones he died to redeem,
Bringing the weary to find rest in him.

Refrain
O Jesus, Lord and Savior, I give myself to thee,
For thou, in thy atonement, didst give thyself for me.
I own no other Master, my heart shall be thy throne.
My life I give, henceforth to live, O Christ, for thee alone.

Lowden had long admired the poetry of Thomas Chisholm. Chisholm was now fifty-one years old and an insurance agent in nearby Vineland, New Jersey. He had already written many uplifting and timeless Christian poems published in *The Pentecostal Herald*. As Lowden studied some of Chisholm's work, he wondered if this man could take Lowden's new ideas and create something special for the "Sunshine's Song" melody.

Chisholm was a Kentuckian by birth and initially made his living teaching in the same one-room schoolhouse he had attended. At twenty-one he became the associate editor of *The Franklin Advocate*, a position he held for five years. In 1893, at the age of twenty-seven, Chisholm was assigned to cover a local revival meeting. Though he went there with no plans other than getting a good newspaper story, Chisholm became a part of his own copy. When the invitation played, he walked the aisle, accepting Christ as his Savior. A few years later Chisholm left journalism to pastor a church in Scottsville, Kentucky, but poor health forced him to resign that position. After recovering from a serious illness, he turned to the insurance trade. Even though he was no longer involved in full-time service, Chisholm continued to compose Christian poetry, some of which Lowden had seen.

In 1917, Chisholm was in his office sorting through mail when he came across a letter from Carl Lowden. He opened the envelope and was surprised to find a request to write lyrics to go with a piece of sheet music that accompanied the letter. Chisholm studied the music for a moment, then picked up a pen and answered the correspondence.

A few days later Lowden received Chisholm's reply. It was not what he expected. His request for lyrics had been turned down. Chisholm had politely informed Lowden he had never

written a poem to music that had already been composed. He had also never written poetry that already had a theme and contained several finished lines. He concluded by stating this was simply not the way he worked.

Being flatly rejected did not faze Lowden. He composed another letter informing Chisholm the initial request had not been a frivolous one. He was also aware it was more than unusual to ask the poet to compose anything in such a constricted format. Yet, Lowden continued, he felt God had led him to Chisholm and that he was the only man who could provide the caliber of lyrics needed for such an obviously inspired tune. He closed by begging Chisholm to rethink his decision.

The second communication touched Chisholm and caused him to reconsider. He still doubted he could create something while working from another writer's notes, but now he decided he would give it a try. It took Chisholm two weeks to come up with lyrics he felt lived up to the song's moving melody.

Lowden was thrilled with Chisholm's new lyrics for "Living for Jesus." Though it was too late for the finished song to be included in the hymnal he had been editing, he used it as the musical centerpiece for the youth conference he was directing. The song made an indelible impression on the teenagers who had gathered at the New Jersey camp. Many of them took "Living for Jesus" back to their home churches in leaflet form, and a few months later the hymn made its publishing debut in the aptly titled *Uplifting Songs*.

At the time it was first published, neither of the writers understood the impact this simple song would have on worship services around the globe. In fact both were shocked when other denominations began to include "Living for Jesus" in their hymnals. The writers were even more stunned when their

hymn became the focal point or theme of Bible studies, books, sermons, and even conventions. Without realizing it, they had hit a chord that struck deeply in the hearts of Christians and had also prompted nonbelievers to take a second look at what the life, death, and resurrection of Jesus really meant.

In his later years Thomas Chisholm modestly looked back at his two most beloved songs, "Great Is Thy Faithfulness" and "Living for Jesus." In trying to sum up the profound effect his hymns had had on so many, he explained, "I have greatly desired that each hymn or poem might send some definite message to the hearts for whom it was written." "Living for Jesus" did that and more. It reminded Christians that they serve a risen Savior who depends upon them to carry on his work on Earth. As is clearly spelled out in this hymn, Easter was not the end, but the beginning. The hope found in the resurrection is still there for all believers to take with them each day they live for Jesus.

The History of
the Easter Egg

*F*or most children it simply would not be Easter without Easter eggs. These brightly colored eggs have long cast their magical spell on little ones during this holiday season. In fact, even before Christ walked the earth, the season of spring and colored eggs were cast together in customs dating all the way back to the ancient Egyptians.

Many early civilizations, including the Persians, Phoenicians, Hindus, and Egyptians, believed the world began as an egg. When that egg was broken, the yellow yolk became the sun, and the remainder made up the earth. The egg was so revered in Egyptian culture that eggs were buried in tombs with the nation's noblemen. The Greeks also buried eggs with their dead. Why did so many ancient cultures attach so much importance to the egg? They realized that the egg was the beginning of life for many creatures. Therefore, each spring, when life was renewed and eggs were laid, the world was given new hope.

It was only natural that the egg would be one of the first symbols of pagan culture that found its way into the Christian celebration of the resurrection. To many of the pagan converts,

the egg represented life. It was an honored symbol of new life. Thus both children and adults viewed the egg with great awe and mystery. When people accepted Christ as their Savior, when they heard the story of his living after having died on the cross, when they understood that he had given them eternal life, the egg naturally came to their minds. So for many new believers, the egg became an important symbol of their faith. To them the egg represented their soul's rebirth.

Long before these new Christians latched onto the egg as a symbol of Easter, their tribes had been partaking in egg hunts. Initially this was done for survival. Eggs were an important food source, and in the times before birds were domesticated, hunters went out looking for whatever type of eggs they could find. They ate eggs from almost every kind of bird, but they often took brightly colored eggs home to give to children as presents. Over time different groups adopted a special day in the spring when their children would participate in a group hunt with other children looking for eggs. The child who found the egg deemed most beautiful and colorful would receive a prize.

In certain parts of Europe, eggs with deep color hues simply did not exist. So, as the custom of children's egg hunts spread, adults would color eggs with dye and hide them the night before the hunt. This added excitement to the game and also made choosing a winner much more difficult. These hunts continued as the various European tribes converted to Christianity, but in many places, the game became a teaching tool.

Orthodox Christians were probably the first to color eggs in ways that created opportunities for explaining the true meaning of Easter. They would first pierce the egg with a needle, completely drain it, and then use bright red paint on the shell. When a child found this fragile egg, they would be asked, "Do

you know why this egg is red?" Then a parent, a church leader, or an older child would explain that the red paint represented the blood of Christ shed for each person's soul.

Over time painting one egg red gave way to using the shell as a canvas. In many places in Eastern Europe, especially in the Dark and Middle Ages, eggs were decorated with images of Christ, his disciples, Mary, Joseph, and other New Testament figures. When all the eggs were gathered, they were laid out in a special order to teach the complete story of the life of Jesus.

Sometime in the Middle Ages in Germany the custom of giving green eggs the day before Good Friday became a tradition. These special eggs symbolizing life were used as decorations on trees. For a while the Easter tree was as important to most German families as the Christmas tree.

In the Scandinavian nations, as well as in some parts of the British Isles, early Christians did not hide eggs. Instead, children would go from house to house begging for brightly colored eggs. To receive an egg, the groups of children would have to act out a portion of the Easter story. Called "Pace egging," from the Hebrew word *Pesach* (Passover), the custom lasted for several hundred years. Over time the eggs became known as "Peace Eggs," representing the peace that Christ could bring to each person's life.

Because eggs were inexpensive in most regions, the practice of decorating Easter eggs crossed all social classes and remained somewhat simple. Yet in Eastern Europe the craft of egg decorating for the holiday was often given over to local artists who created striped or patterned eggs, often using a rainbow of colors. These elaborate displays brought out competitive rivalries, and soon the final product included gold, silver, and even jewels. Still, for many children the thrill of finding

an egg had nothing to do with the decorated shells; they just wanted to have the opportunity to enjoy a treat.

In medieval times eggs were on the list of foods that could not be eaten during the season of Lent. This meant that for more than six weeks, children could not enjoy one of their favorite foods. Thus, when they were given the opportunity to finally hunt for hard-boiled eggs, they sought them out as if they were treasure. The first few rarely made it home; they were consumed where they were found.

At first many children simply used a hat or an old sack when they gathered eggs. This often meant that a number of eggs arrived home broken. To save the eggs, families began to use a basket. Originally the basket was meant for taking food to church on Easter morning to be blessed by the priest. This custom of having food blessed in God's house actually can be traced back to the Old Testament. Once the basket was home and the food had been removed, families began to allow their children to use it during their egg hunts. Soon craftsmen began to create baskets resembling a bird's nest. These special Easter baskets were kept and passed down from generation to generation and probably represent the first successful commercial exploitation of the holiday.

Easter eggs fell upon hard times not long after Martin Luther broke off from the Catholic Church. New Protestant splinter denominations in Western Europe and England felt that anything having pagan roots should be removed from the Christian church. Thus, groups like the Puritans banned both Christmas and Easter. For several hundred years generations of children grew up knowing nothing about this ancient tradition.

In the middle of the nineteenth century, Easter made a comeback as Protestant churches in England and the United States

began to again recognize the day. The tradition of colored eggs also returned to the forefront of the holiday at this time. During the Civil War, President Lincoln oversaw an egg-rolling contest on the Capitol grounds. This Monday-after-Easter custom has continued and is now held on the White House grounds.

Though the use of eggs at Easter can be traced back to the origins of the holiday, the most famous decorated eggs are much more modern. In the last years of the nineteenth century, the famed artist Fabergé created one gold-and-jewel encrusted egg each year to give to the family of the Russian czar. Eventually the number was upped to two, and these rare eggs, complete with surprises hidden inside, remain the most famous Easter eggs in the world. Today Fabergé eggs are considered priceless.

The incredible value of the Fabergé eggs notwithstanding, the meaning that new Christians found when this once mystical pagan icon was transformed into a symbol of faith is worth much more. As much as eggs represent a recurring cycle of life, the Easter egg was adopted by Christians to signify the eternal life that was theirs when they accepted Christ as their Savior. Thus, more than eighteen hundred years after it first became associated with this special holiday, the Easter egg can still teach a powerful lesson of faith.

Lead Me to Calvary

ne of the questions often asked of tour guides in Israel is "When can we see Calvary?" Many visitors are disappointed when they discover they can only view where historians and theologians think Christ was crucified or believe he was buried. Guides simply cannot point out any existing landmarks from the crucifixion or the resurrection. They must guess the locations of the cross and the tomb. So in a sense, when Jennie Evelyn Hussey wrote her poem, "Lead Me to Calvary," she could not have been thinking of a physical landmark; after all, she lived her whole life without journeying very far from her New England home. Hussey was instead speaking of the location of the spiritual Calvary. During her eighty-four years of life, this woman could have easily guided anyone to that monumental place of hope, faith, and life. This trip could be made by simply following her example.

Hussey was a bright, energetic person who seemed to possess the rare combination of talent and charisma. Born on February 8, 1874, in Henniker, New Hampshire, she grew up in a Quaker family who understood the value of service to God and man. The Husseys by their faith were peaceful people, but they took the Quaker lifestyle much further than just opposing

war. They were a compassionate family who tried to live out Christ's commandments each day of their lives. Neighbors and friends knew the Husseys would always be there in times of need, with both sharing and support. This family exemplified the way Christians are supposed to live, and this standard of faith was not lost on their daughter.

A thin girl with dark, sparkling eyes, Jennie Hussey smiled easily and walked with a light step. From her grammar school days, she realized that studying and asking questions were the best ways to get answers. So while outwardly carefree, she was also a deep thinker who challenged others around her at both church and school. Besides being curious by nature, Hussey was also a talented writer. As many of her era did, she leaned toward poetry over prose, spending many hours crafting verses that captured snapshots from her life. Most of those who read her poems predicted she would one day leave Henniker to attend college. Some even believed she might be the next Emily Dickinson. Yet fate put a huge roadblock in Hussey's career path.

Jennie had a sister who was an invalid. It is unknown exactly what was the problem with the sibling, only that she was unable to take care of herself. Someone had to be with her constantly, seeing to her every need. When Jennie's parents died, this task fell on the young woman.

Most in Hussey's situation would have looked for a way out. She didn't. She gladly accepted her challenge even though it meant giving up dreams of her own. So for almost all the rest of her years, Hussey's life was not her own; it belonged almost completely to her sister. For decades she worked tirelessly from early in the morning until late at night. In the midst of her long days, friends would come by and visit. They were amazed when she always greeted them with a smile and an uplifting story.

They had come to comfort her, but they always left having been comforted and inspired by her.

In what little free time she had, Hussey continued to write poetry. As the years went by, more and more of those poems centered on her faith. She honestly believed that by caring for her sister she was living out God's plan for her life. When her friends asked how she endured the job thrust upon her, Hussey explained there was a joy in service that could be found nowhere else. Hence, when she served her sister, she felt as if she were serving Christ. She thought of her life as a gift that allowed her to follow as closely as possible in her Savior's footsteps.

One of the verses Hussey often shared with others was Luke 9:23: "And he said to them all, If any man will come after me, let him deny himself, and take up his cross daily, and follow me." Though she lived this verse each day of her life, she often told others she felt it was not enough. She desired to do even more, to touch even more lives. Thus she wrote poems encouraging friends and family to embrace the fullness of a life of Christian service.

Hussey was in her mid-forties, when, after reading the Bible and contemplating the nature of her faith, inspiration hit her. As she prayed, a vision of Christ on the cross appeared to her. Picking up pen and paper, she began a poem that would find its way from her heart to hearts all around the globe. These short verses would allow Hussey to go beyond her own small town and share her talent with the world.

"Lead Me to Calvary" was Jennie's testimony. It was what put the smile on her face and drove the bitterness from her heart. It is the reason she never felt cheated by the life of service she had been forced to live. One verse is especially personal and biographical.

Lead Me to Calvary

King of my life I crown thee now
Thine shall the glory be;
Lest I forget thy thorn-crowned brow,
Lead me to Calvary.

Show me the tomb where thou wast laid,
Tenderly mourned and wept;
Angels in robes of light arrayed
Guarded thee whilst thou slept.

Let me like Mary, through the gloom,
Come with a gift to thee;
Show to me now the empty tomb,
Lead me to Calvary.

May I be willing, Lord, to bear
Daily the cross for thee;
Even thy cup of grief to share
Thou hast borne all for me.

Refrain
Lest I forget Gethsemane,
Lest I forget thine agony,
Lest I forget thy love for me,
Lead me to Calvary.

May I be willing, Lord, to bear
Daily the cross for thee;
Even thy cup of grief to share
Thou hast borne all for me.

As with most of her works, she initially shared this poem with her church. Many of the members were so deeply touched by "Lead Me to Calvary" that they encouraged Hussey to submit it for publication. Soon Hussey's words found their way into the hands of one of the nation's foremost gospel music publishers, William J. Kirkpatrick.

Like many born in the first half of the nineteenth century, Kirkpatrick was the son of immigrants. Born in Pennsylvania in 1838, he was an accomplished musician who, when still a child, was proficient on the flute and violin. A veteran of the Civil War, he returned from the service to work in the furniture business. His only contact with Christian music during this time was when he led singing in church or at revival. His week-to-week routine might have continued in this fashion if not for his wife's sudden death in 1878.

Kirkpatrick was forty years old and a widower. Suddenly aware of the fragility of life, he decided to leave his stable job and pursue his love of music on a full-time basis. His first step was becoming the music director at Philadelphia's Grace Methodist Episcopal Church. Soon thereafter he also joined with John R. Sweney and formed a gospel music publishing company. This dual occupation led to his not only directing and editing music but composing it as well. Over the next four decades Kirkpatrick composed the melodies to such beloved standards as "Coming Home," "Jesus Saves," and "Redeemed."

When Kirkpatrick first glanced at Jennie Hussey's "Lead Me to Calvary," he was well past the age of retirement. Though he was elderly, his keen eye had not faded nor had his ability to write music that perfectly matched the mood and message of another's lyrics. Thus, with a great deal of reverence he sat down to score Hussey's work.

Kirkpatrick's tune was almost gentle in tone, much like Hussey's spirit, but there was also a subtle strength in the easy-to-sing melody. Though dealing with one of the most tragic moments in history, the music possessed a positive, almost upbeat nature. In this way it reflected the life and personality of the lyricist. One of the final songs Kirkpatrick published before his death in 1921, "Lead Me to Calvary" was also quickly recognized as one of his best.

Thanks to Hussey's descriptive lyrics, most Christians, even if they have never been to the Holy Land, can clearly picture this scene when they sing "Lead Me to Calvary." Yet this popular hymn is more than just Easter imagery; it challenges all believers to search their hearts and evaluate how much of Calvary can be found there. Everyone who looked at Jennie Hussey could see she had embraced the example of the man who died for her sins; she gladly lived a life of service and devotion and happily accepted the call she had been given. Hussey's faith led her to Calvary, and once she was there, she never left.

25

*H*e Lives!

*A*lfred Ackley was in the midst of a weeklong revival in 1934 at which those who turned out were by and large looking for answers and comfort. The Great Depression had all but wiped them out. Many men had lost their jobs, while the lucky ones who still had employment were wondering if their jobs would last until the end of the year. A new president had promised that help was on the way, but for the moment those seemed like hollow words as the bleak times continued. For many the only place to turn to find any hope at all was God. So in revivals across the country, thousands were filling churches, theaters, auditoriums, and tents looking for answers.

During this bleak season, Ackley was one of the evangelists called upon to speak all across the country. His mission was to steer the lost to Christ and bring comfort and hope to hurting believers. Though he had more than twenty years' experience as a pastor and Christian leader, the task he now faced was anything but routine or easy. Despair seemed to be permanently etched on many of the faces that looked up at him night after night. That hopelessness often seemed to descend on the services like a storm cloud on a summer afternoon.

Beyond being a preacher, Ackley was a musician. He not only spoke the Word; he also sang it. His father had passed on this passion for music to him in the late 1800s. Ackley was so gifted he soon outgrew home instruction and traveled from Spring Hill, Pennsylvania, to New York City to study harmony and composition with Hans Kronald. In the Big Apple, an Englishman noticed Ackley's talents and took stories of the young man's abilities back to his homeland. A few months later Ackley was given the opportunity to move to London and attend the Royal Academy of Music. He devoted much of the time in the UK to studying cello.

Ackley felt a call to be more than just a musician, and just before World War I he attended Westminster Theological Seminary, where he obtained a degree in 1914. He began his ministry at a Presbyterian Church in Wilkes-Barre, Pennsylvania. Over the next few years he also pastored churches in Pittsburgh and Escondido, California. Then came two opportunities of a lifetime. Famed evangelist Billy Sunday asked Ackley to be his crusade pianist, and the Rodeheaver Publishing Company offered him a job as a music editor. For the next twenty years, Ackley appeared at thousands of services, wrote scores of songs, and studied theology in great depth. During this time he became recognized as more than just a fabulously talented musician; he also earned a reputation as a top biblical scholar. Thus many pastors came to Ackley with questions few theologians would attempt to answer. Yet none of those complex questions compared to one a young man asked Ackley at this 1934 revival. This single query would test the evangelist's education and experience like nothing had ever tested them before.

Each night of the revival, Ackley noted a young man in the audience who came alone and sat well away from others in

the crowd. The visitor listened intently but showed no signs of understanding either the message or the music. He also never came forward to ask a question, seek prayer, or make a decision for Christ. Yet he was always back the next evening.

On the final night of the revival, the young man was there again. Ackley noticed him as he took the podium. As Ackley spoke on the divine presence of Jesus in the daily lives of believers, the young man's eyes lit up. Ackley could even see this excitement from the pulpit. Yet when the invitation was played, the young man still did not join the others who came forward to accept Christ as their Savior. In fact, he disappeared.

Thirty minutes later the crowd had dispersed and Ackley was also getting ready to leave when a voice stopped him. Turning, the evangelist was greeted by the young man he had noticed earlier. The stranger's expression was intense and his body coiled tight with suppressed rage.

"I have to know something," the stranger barked.

"Yes," the evangelist quietly replied.

"Why," he demanded, "should I worship a dead Jew?"

The question stunned Ackley. No one had ever asked it before. For a moment he thought about how to answer, then he felt a sudden rush of energy and blurted out, "He lives! I tell you, he is not dead, but lives here and now! Jesus Christ is more alive today than ever before. I can prove it by my own experience, as well as the testimony of countless others."

Excitement flowed through his body as Ackley stared intently into the young man's eyes. The visitor's rage was gone, replaced by a sense of surprise. He was now ready to listen, and Ackley was ready to witness. Signaling toward two chairs, the evangelist sat down and shared his own story with the young man. When their conversation ended, they prayed together. Each left

He Lives!

I serve a risen Savior,
He's in the world today;
I know that he is living,
Whatever men may say;
I see his hand of mercy,
I hear his voice of cheer,
And just the time I need him,
He's always near.

In all the world around me
I see his loving care,
And though my heart grows weary,
I never will despair;
I know that he is leading
Through all the stormy blast,
The day of his appearing
Will come at last.

Rejoice, rejoice, O Christian,
Lift up your voice and sing
Eternal hallelujahs
To Jesus Christ the King!
The hope of all who seek him,
The help of all who find,
None other is so loving,
So good and kind.

Refrain
He lives, he lives,
Christ Jesus lives today!
He walks with me and talks with me
Along life's narrow way.
He lives, he lives,
Salvation to impart!
You ask me how I know he lives?
He lives within my heart.

knowing that belief in a living Christ was a tie that would bind them through this life and the next.

The words that began Ackley's straightforward reply to the young man's question stuck with the pastor throughout the night. Like a tune he couldn't get out of his head, a silent voice only he could hear kept repeating "he lives" over and over again. Unable to sleep, unable to read, and unable even to pray, Ackley got up and found a piano. Sitting down, he repeated over and over again "he lives" as his fingers randomly ran across the keyboard. In mere minutes a tune as well as lyrics formed in his head. He later said, "The thought of his ever-living presence brought the music promptly and easily. The words followed immediately." Within half an hour Ackley was singing, "He lives! He lives! Christ Jesus lives today, he walks with me, and talks with me along life's narrow way. He lives! He lives! Salvation to impart; you ask me how I know he lives? He lives within my heart!"

Being on the editorial board of one of the major gospel music publishers allowed Ackley to immediately put "He Lives!" before the public. Also, Billy Sunday's featuring it in his crusades helped the new work's exposure. Thus, within just a few years, Ackley's answer to the question, "Why should I worship a dead Jew?" found its way into almost every new American hymnal. Taken abroad by American servicemen and women, by the end of World War II the song was also well known around the globe.

A song that begins "I serve a risen Savior" is naturally fitted to the Easter season. Though there is no mention of the cross, this hymn is one that defines the hope found when the empty tomb of Christ was discovered. "He lives," the disciples quickly realized, and they told others, "Christ lives!" And he lived not just in those days after he was crucified, but he lives on to this

day. Alfred Ackley used his belief in that fact to lead a young man to Christ. Because of a sinner who came to understand the importance of the resurrection, a song was born that still brings others to the knowledge of a risen Savior. Hundreds of millions know what Alfred Ackley believed and set to music; it simply can't be Easter unless "He Lives."

The History of the Easter Bunny

The advent of both Santa Claus as a Christmas symbol and eggs as an Easter icon can be traced to Christian roots and beliefs. The Easter bunny is a different animal altogether. No connection exists between this endearing children's character and any element of the Christian faith. Yet for many children, the Easter bunny is a wonderful reminder of the coming of Easter.

For thousands of years rabbits have been considered to have mystical powers. Many cultures that built statues of fertility gods and goddesses gave them rabbit heads. Certainly, few creatures reproduce as often or in as great a number as do rabbits, so this association seems natural. The bunny's first link with Easter probably sprang from a story about one of these ancient deities.

Oestre, a pagan goddess from which the name *Easter* might have been derived, played an important part in spring celebrations. Many European tribes thought that she actually drove winter away and reawakened the world for its annual rebirth in spring. A legend, passed from one generation to the next,

told of Oestre giving an audience to a bird. The bird looked into Oestre's face and was overcome with the beauty it saw in the goddess's rabbit-like features. Sensing the special nature of the rabbit, the bird asked the goddess to transform him into a rabbit. Oestre acted upon the request the next spring. When the bird became a rabbit, it forgot everything about its former life except how to lay eggs. This bird's eggs were then gathered by Oestre and presented to the world's best children. This story is the first known connection of the rabbit and the egg. Over time, the tale was embellished to the point where the rabbit's eggs were made of gold.

When people who had worshiped Oestre and other pagan gods became Christians, the story of the bird that became a rabbit all but disappeared. Only in a few remote villages in Germany did a bunny find its way into Easter lore. In fact, there probably would have been no Easter bunny if not for the large numbers of rabbits that populated so much of Europe.

In the Middle Ages, Easter egg hunts usually took place in open fields or meadows. Children who sought the hidden eggs regularly frightened rabbits concealed in the grass. As eggs were often discovered in the same location from which the bunnies had just fled, children naturally associated their newly found colored treasure with the furry animals. In time this resulted in stories of a rabbit laying the colorful eggs. For children who loved fantasy, and for parents who felt a desire to bring some fun into their kids' lives, the tale seemed perfect. Soon adults even told children that the best place to find Easter eggs was in a rabbit's nest.

Germany was the first place the Easter bunny appeared in stories. Several books published as early as the sixteenth century connected the rabbit to the holiday. In the early 1800s,

German candy makers sensed the great commercial possibilities offered by the rabbit's association with the holiday. Using a variety of recipes, numerous shops created a wide range of edible bunnies. In large part because of the popularity of these treats, in Germany the Easter bunny stopped laying eggs and started delivering candy.

Dutch and German immigrants brought the Easter bunny to the United States as Oschter Haws, a large, white hare. This mythical creature brought beautiful eggs to those who had been good all year long. To prepare for his visit, children would make nests in hay or place hats or bonnets in the barn where the white rabbit would leave his bounty. Thus, for some immigrant children, Oschter Haws was the spring equivalent of Santa Claus. When Americans started celebrating Easter in the mid to late 1800s, Oschter Haws became the Easter bunny. Stories were written about this benevolent rabbit. Department stores even had employees dress up in bunny suits to lure shoppers. Yet, at this time, it was still the holiday candy that proved the most popular element of the old German Easter rabbit tradition.

Beatrix Potter's famous children's stories that began with *The Tale of Peter Rabbit* owe a bit of their inspiration to the acceptance of the Easter bunny; surely so does that cartoon icon Bugs Bunny. Yet what really cemented the holiday hare into a prominent role in Easter festivities was a hit single recorded by Gene Autry in 1950. Autry had scored huge seasonal hits with "Rudolph, the Red-Nosed Reindeer" and "Here Comes Santa Claus," so the singing cowboy had a strong holiday track record. Thanks to his Western movies and radio shows, he was also beloved by millions of children. Thus, when Steve Nelsom and Jack Rollins penned a song about a rabbit named Peter Cottontail, they asked Autry to sing it. His recording of

"Peter Cottontail" became a huge hit and launched a marketing bonanza. Soon there were Peter Cottontail coloring books, story-books, pajamas, and even dishes. Peter Cottontail appeared at stores and posed for pictures with children. A generation later television got on board, and Peter hippity-hopped his way into a new set of hearts. So Autry's hit song, and all that resulted in its wake, no doubt made the bunny a permanent star in every Easter celebration.

A recent poll showed that almost 90 percent of Americans include the Easter bunny in their holiday celebrations. So while it is true that this furry symbol has no links to the events of the first Easter, he has opened up a world of opportunity for Christians to share what happened on a cross and in a tomb two thousand years ago. The Easter bunny has taken the holiday to a host of new non-Christian people. Once they share Easter with this rabbit, maybe they will dig deeper and discover the real reason for the season.

29

Because He Lives

*I*n a little more than three decades, "Because He Lives" has become one of the world's favorite hymns. The product of the incredible talents of Bill and Gloria Gaither, this unique song has accomplished something very rare; it is a Southern gospel standard that has been accepted into the hymnals of almost all the world's major Christian denominations. Though it is sung around the year, "Because He Lives" has also become one of the most popular hymns performed during the Easter season. And like the holiday itself, this sacred classic tells a story of hopelessness and death giving way to life and light. It is a song about new birth, new hope, and a new world. As much as any centuries-old standard, "Because He Lives" captures all the emotion and wonder of Easter.

The story of this song begins in the American heartland, in the community of Alexandria, Indiana. In the middle of the Midwest, two high school teachers married and began to work on a dream that became a calling. Though Bill had roots in Southern gospel music, Bill and Gloria Gaither wrote music that appealed to a much broader audience. In time the songwriting duo constructed a bridge between inspirational gospel music and what was to become contemporary Christian music. This

couple therefore did not just write new hymns; they revolutionized the Christian music industry. Some critics have even been so bold as to say, "The Gaithers brought God out of the closet." With one song in the last year of the turbulent sixties, they might have done just that and, in the process, given the world one of its mightiest Easter anthems. However, that incredible gift of music was not all that was on Bill and Gloria's minds at the time. In 1969, they were looking at the chaos of the era and wondering if God himself might have given up on the world. In that cold winter, Bill and Gloria had been able to give up their day jobs to devote their lives to music. Yet even though their careers were solid and their names had become well known in the music industry, their days were not as bright as their musical prospects. The Indiana winter had been a long, hard one. For months snow had been piled on top of snow everywhere the couple looked. The skies rarely cleared and the north wind seemed even more fierce than usual.

The Gaithers figured that when spring finally arrived, things would brighten. After all, Easter was coming, a time of new birth and new hope. Yet while Gloria grew more excited by the prospects of the changing season, Bill's spiritual and creative slump continued even as new flowers bloomed and they celebrated the resurrection of their Lord.

Bill needed answers. He had faced a period of personal loss in his family and challenges with his health. He needed to escape the haze of doubt and fear that seemed to hem him in at every turn. Together, Bill and Gloria saw the world in which they lived filled with uncertainty. They were not alone. Millions of Americans felt the same way. A decade of social unrest, the reality of the divide between races, pain caused by the needed integration of schools and society, growing dissatisfaction with

the war in Vietnam, countless bestselling books trumpeting the end times, inflation and unemployment, and the mood among many young people that God was either dead or did not care about them had killed the generally optimistic nature of most Americans. Countless souls, overwhelmed by what they perceived as constant bad news, had turned to drugs, alcohol, and sex. The older generation felt that the country's best days were in the past, and their baby boomer children agreed. Yet both groups thought the other was to blame. Perhaps because of this, the voice of the young — rock music — was often depressing. Frighteningly, the established church seemed to have no more answers than did the politicians in Washington. Cynicism was alive and growing in almost every home in America. Ironically, it was during this period that Bill and Gloria discovered they were expecting a baby. This was wonderful news that excited them both, but even while celebrating, they wondered if it was really a wise thing to bring a baby into such a chaotic world.

One sunny day, at their small A-frame offices, Bill, Gloria, and George, Bill's father, walked over the paved parking lot. George Gaither, in his unassuming way, walked with Bill and Gloria to show them a spot that they had not noticed. The elder man pointed out a tiny blade of grass which had pushed aside layers of dirt, rock, and concrete to reach the sunshine of the world that lay above. This tiny plant had such a strong will to live that it had overcome all the odds to fulfill its destiny. The miracle that George had discovered in the parking lot became a symbol to Bill and Gloria of the truth that life will win even in the bleakest circumstances.

On July 19, 1970, Benjamin Gaither was born. Although Bill and Gloria knew the world would not be a perfect place for

their new baby, their faith had been renewed. They began to see reminders that Christ had entered a world of chaos and had brought peace and understanding. Just like the blade of grass, those who had faith would survive and grow stronger in this time as well. Mary probably had her own doubt and fears about what her son faced in the world, but ultimately she watched that same world transformed through the actions of the Prince of Peace.

In an inspired moment, Gloria began a song expressing the hope that life can be lived with confidence because he lives! The song she wrote that day was shaped by the birth of a son, and her now renewed faith in God.

After the event of Good Friday, the disciples and other followers of Jesus must have felt a great deal like Bill and Gloria did in the winter of 1969. These men and women who had known Jesus as a friend and companion had to have been confused. With his death their world suddenly filled with doubt and their questions were coming much faster than their answers. Yet imagine their reaction when they saw the living Christ, the Savior who had escaped the tomb. Their perspective had suddenly and dramatically changed, because he lives.

Like "Amazing Grace" and "Battle Hymn of the Republic," "Because He Lives" is a classic piece of music that appeals to everyone going through periods of great doubt and fear. As long as the world is a chaotic place, "Because He Lives" will remain a treasured musical message of hope and faith and therefore an Easter favorite.

28

*T*en Thousand
Angels Cried

*I*n 2001, during a memorial service for firefighters who lost their lives during the September 11 terrorist attack on New York and Washington, David Patillo turned on the television and heard his composition "Ten Thousand Angels Cried" being used to honor these fallen heroes. In the wake of the most horrible event of a new century, the Texarkana songwriter's composition was bringing hope to many who had been crushed by the events of 9/11.

The moving anthem was born ten years before. Patillo, then a young man from Texarkana, Arkansas, was listening to a gospel concert at a Church of the Nazarene on the Texas side of the city. The year 1991 marked the seventieth anniversary of the Speer Family's first performance. During those seven decades, several generations of Speers had appeared all around the world and sold millions of records, creating a loyal following that few groups in any genre could touch. While always spending a portion of each concert performing traditional gospel music, they also devoted a segment to more contemporary songs. In fact

they had been one of the first groups to latch onto the music of Bill and Gloria Gaither, thus opening the door for this husband and wife's contributions to Christian music. Yet on this occasion, the Speers did not introduce a new gospel song but instead were the spark that stirred a songwriter to compose a dynamic Easter tribute.

On that night, David Patillo's inspirational creative fire was stoked when Ben, Brock, and the rest of the Speers dusted off a song they had first heard three decades before. The group's rendition of Ray Overholt's "Ten Thousand Angels" was sincerely appreciated by most of the audience, but the applause it drew was not lengthy. In fact, it was quickly forgotten as the group wrapped its harmonies around more familiar standards such as "God Gave the Song" and "The King Is Coming." Yet Patillo didn't hear the songs that followed "Ten Thousand Angels." The young man was so caught up in the message of "Ten Thousand Angels" that everything and everyone around him simply disappeared. The Speers' performance had taken him to a new place, and in that place he quickly found a much deeper understanding of the first Easter.

"I had heard my mom sing 'Ten Thousand Angels' as a kid," David explained in his soft Southern drawl. "I really thought it was a great song. Yet as I listened to the Speers sing it, the song hit me from a different perspective. You know the Scripture mentions natural phenomena, weather and stuff like that, and after Jesus was crucified how the sky was darkened. Yet it never said in the Scripture that it rained. As I listened to the song this time I was almost there, at the crucifixion, in my mind." At that moment, in the cascading myriad of David's thoughts, it was raining at Calvary too.

Looking around in the pew, David spotted an offering envelope. Picking it up, he grabbed a short pencil he spied beside a hymnal. Now inspired and fully armed with the necessary tools of the songwriter's trade, he felt a need to take the theme he heard in Overholt's "Ten Thousand Angels" in a new direction. Completely tuning out the Speers' beautiful harmonies, David focused solely on thoughts of the day when Jesus was nailed to the cross.

"You can't just stay in one place in your mind," he explained about the songwriting process, "so here I was reliving the Passion of Christ in my mind. I am thinking about the angels, and then it takes a different perspective. You know everyone thinks of angels as these wonderful little white-clad creatures sitting around with peaceful looks on their faces, but the Scripture talks about angels actually being very fierce and capable of great strength. In the Old Testament it talks about one angel annihilating a whole army. Then I thought, 'Good grief, [with] all this power [at his disposal], he could have called twelve legions of angels.' It then hit me, Jesus was the Word, but without the signal or the word from Jesus, the angels were not going to make that move. They were not going to make that call to take him down from the cross on their own. They had to wait for Christ."

Though no one around him knew it, David was no longer at a gospel concert; he had traveled back in time to the most horrific moment in history. The songwriter could now clearly see Jesus on the cross. Even as a spirited performance played all around him, he heard none of it. At that moment it was as if he were standing right in front of the cross at Calvary. This vision was so real that David could see Christ's face, and he witnessed the pain of that moment. He also now fully realized that Jesus had

made the choice to give his life for sinners. There were legions of angels waiting to save him, and yet he chose to suffer for man. Patillo had never been so moved or awed by this stark vision of Easter. "All of these thoughts were playing together in my mind," David recalled, "and I realized that the angels' awesome strength must have given way to awesome emotion. Unable to act, they must have begun to cry. They knew their job was not to take him down, but just to be witnesses. As they began to cry in my scenario, then their tears appeared to be rain."

David finished the song the same day he conceived it. Yet because of the emotions that were a part of his vision, it was to be several weeks before he could sing it to anyone.

"Trying to sing it was simply too emotional for me," he explained. "Every time I tried I started crying and couldn't get through it. Finally, a few weeks later, when I could sing it, those who listened told me I had written something special."

Though David performed gospel music in many churches in the South, he was not a well-known songwriter, so he couldn't just send a demo off to gospel record producers and wait to see who would line up to record his latest composition. In fact the only person who jumped at the chance at cutting Patillo's "Ten Thousand Angels Cried" was David. He put it out on a local Texarkana label, and the song received limited airplay on gospel stations. Yet, for reasons the songwriter didn't fully understand, the song didn't simply fade away. It was still played enough that a few other recording artists heard it. One even decided to cut it.

Karen Peck was a popular Southern gospel artist and a regular on Bill Gaither's Homecoming tours. When she heard Patillo's song, she opted to not only record it but also to release it as a single. With *Touched by an Angel* racking up huge ratings

on TV and Billy Graham and several other writers using angels as subjects for bestselling books, it seemed perfect timing for "Ten Thousand Angels Cried." Not surprisingly, Peck's strong and deeply spiritual version of Patillo's dramatic song quickly landed in gospel music's top ten. Yet this success paled in comparison to what lay just around the corner.

David was still enjoying Karen Peck's cut of his song when he got a call from pop singer LeAnn Rimes's family. The teen sensation, one of the nation's hottest popular and country music vocalists, wanted to put "Ten Thousand Angels Cried" onto her gospel album, "You Light Up My Life." This move forever changed David's career and paved the way for his song becoming one of the most popular Easter anthems of the next century.

Rimes's album sold five million copies and earned the unique status of being the first Christian record to top the pop, country, and Christian charts at the same time. Though not released as a single, "Ten Thousands Angels Cried" still garnered a great deal of airplay. This led to Patillo's song landing in songbooks, finding its way onto other artists' albums, and even being written into several Easter musicals. Yet even more amazing, by 2000, Patillo's musical take on the passion of Christ had become one of the most popular Easter hymns performed in churches all around the world. Musical tracks for the song continually topped sales charts each spring. For many, Good Friday and Easter sunrise services were not complete until someone sang the lines, "I've never seen ten thousand angels cry, but I'm sure they did as they stood by and watched a Savior die." Suddenly, thanks to the message found in "Ten Thousands Angels Cried," many people realized that Good Friday was a day when sadness not only filled the earth but the heavens too. The song's

simple lines are so filled with imagery and emotion that they invite the historical Easter to come alive and take root in individual souls. Three hundred years earlier, this personal take on faith was what Isaac Watts felt worship needed, and with "Ten Thousand Angels Cried," David Patillo brought it alive as few others ever had.

In 2005, Patillo picked up the phone and found himself talking to Ray Overholt, the writer of the song that inspired Patillo's song. Now in his eighties and blind, Overholt wanted David to know that he had been deeply moved by the new song and was honored that his own "Ten Thousand Angels" had inspired it. Now both men fully understood that through a Speer Family performance God had brought them together in a very special way for a very special purpose.

Since LeAnn Rimes took "Ten Thousand Angels Cried" to the world, more than 250 artists have recorded David Patillo's songs. He has charted twenty-five times in gospel music performing his own music. Yet he will probably never again write a song that will have the lasting impact of "Ten Thousand Angels Cried." With his new take on the events of the crucifixion, Patillo created an Easter hymn that seems destined to inspire Christians for generations — a song so rich in emotion that it takes root in the heart and never leaves.

Stories Behind the Hymns That Inspire America

Songs That Unite Our Nation

Ace Collins, Author of the Bestselling *Stories Behind the Best-Loved Songs of Christmas*

From the moment the pilgrims landed on the shores of the New World, to the dark days following September 11th, songs of faith have inspired, comforted, and rallied our beloved country. *Stories Behind the Hymns That Inspire America* describes the people, places, and events that have shaped the heart and soul of America. The stories behind these songs will fascinate you and bring new meaning and richness to special spiritual moments in the history of our nation.

The songs in this book have energized movements, illuminated dark paths, commemorated historic events, taken the message of freedom and faith across this nation and beyond, healed broken spirits, and righted wrongs. Their stories will make you proud of your heritage as you realize anew that in America, even one voice can have a lasting influence.

Hardcover, Jacketed: 0-310-24879-5

Pick up a copy today at your favorite bookstore!

Stories Behind the Great Traditions of Christmas

Ace Collins

The cheer of a crackling hearth fire.

Colorful cards from friends and loved ones.

An evergreen tree festooned with ornaments.

The golden traditions of Christmas—gifts, wreaths, stockings, carols, mistletoe, and more—infuse our celebration of the season with meaning and glowing memories. And, in ways you may not realize, they point us to the birth of Christ.

Stories Behind the Great Traditions of Christmas reveals the people, places, and events that shaped the best-loved customs of this merriest of holidays. Here are spiritual insights, true-life tales, and captivating legends to intrigue you and your family and bring new luster and depth to your celebration of Jesus' birth.

The traditions of Christmas lend beauty, awe, and hope to the holiday, causing people all over the world to anticipate it with joy. The stories in this book will warm your heart as you rediscover the true and eternal significance of Christmas.

Hardcover, Jacketed: 0-310-24880-9

Pick up a copy today at your favorite bookstore!

Stories Behind the Best-Loved Songs of Christmas

Ace Collins

Following in the successful footsteps of our *Christmas Carols Miniature Edition* (more than 300,000 sold), this lovely little adaptation of a popular book about the origins of more than thirty of the most beloved Christmas songs, both secular and religious, promises to be a strong seller as well. "Collins is an ace at song history," notes *Booklist*.

Hardcover, Miniature: 0-310-80757-3

Pick up a copy today at your favorite bookstore!

ZONDERVAN®
.com

More Stories Behind the Best-Loved Songs of Christmas

Ace Collins, Bestselling Author

Ace Collins has dug deep to uncover the true stories behind your favorite Christmas songs. Explore how these songs came into being, and discover a deeper appreciation for these melodic messages of peace, hope, and joy that celebrate the birth of Jesus.

Hardcover, Jacketed: 0-310-26314-X

Pick up a copy today at your favorite bookstore!

I Saw Him in Your Eyes

Everyday People Making
Extraordinary Impact in the
Lives of Karen Kingsbury,
Terri Blackstock, Bobby
Bowden, Charlie Daniels,
S. Truett Cathy, and More

Ace Collins

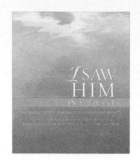

This collection of moving stories reveals the power of
ordinary people to shape the lives of others in unexpected,
sometimes astonishing ways. Bestselling author Ace Collins
presents the inspiring recollections of some of America's
best-loved leaders. These uplifting personal accounts reveal
the life-changing impact of a simple kind act, of a good
word spoken at the right time, of an everyday life whose
unassuming character makes all the difference in someone
else's world.

These real-life stories will encourage you, uplift you, and fill
you with gratitude for those who have touched your own life.
And they will cause you to consider how your own ordinary
life influences someone else in an extraordinary way.

Softcover: 0-310-26318-2

Pick up a copy today at your favorite bookstore!

Turn Your Radio On

The Stories Behind Gospel Music's All-Time Greatest Songs

Ace Collins

Turn Your Radio On tells the fascinating stories behind gospel music's most unforgettable songs, including "Amazing Grace," "The Battle Hymn of the Republic," "He Touched Me," "I'll Fly Away," "Were You There?" and many more. These are the songs that have shaped our faith and brought us joy. You'll find out:

- What famous song traces back to a sailor's desperate prayer.
- What Bill Gaither tune was recorded by Elvis Presley in 1969—and won a Grammy.
- What song was born during a carriage ride through Washington, D.C., at the onset of the Civil War.

Turn Your Radio On is an inspiring journey through the songs that are part of the roots of our faith today.

Softcover: 0-310-21153-0

Pick up a copy today at your favorite bookstore!

ZONDERVAN®
.com

The Cathedrals

The Story of America's Best-Loved Gospel Quartet

from the founding members Glen Payne and George Younce with Ace Collins

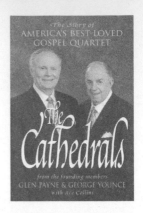

For more than thirty years the Cathedrals, America's most popular male quartet, have told the gospel in song from London to New York, from the Holy Land to Nashville. They have appeared on *The Today Show*, *Prime Time Country*, and almost every Bill Gaither "Old Friends" special. They have sung with orchestras and renowned choirs, and opened up southern gospel music to millions who had never heard it before they heard the Cathedrals.

The Cathedrals tells the inside story of this beloved gospel group and the two men whose voices have helped make it famous. From early struggles on the road to the heights of popularity, here's the heartwarming, firsthand account of their amazing success and longevity. Scores of black-and-white and color photos chronicle changes over the years, while lyrics from the most popular songs show you why the music of the Cathedrals has charmed audiences for more than three decades.

Hardcover, Jacketed: 0-310-20983-8

Pick up a copy today at your favorite bookstore!

We want to hear from you. Please send your comments about this book to us in care of zreview@zondervan.com. Thank you.